THE LIGHT OF MUH...

A Child's Version of
Muhammad ﷺ the Messenger of Islam

by
Hajjah Amina Adil

Retold By Karima Sperling
and
Illustrated by Alia Sperling

Naqshbandi-Haqqani Sufi Order of America

ISBN: 1-930409-41-9

Library of Congress Cataloging-in-Publication Data

Adil, Hajjah Amina.
The light of Muhammad : a child's version of Muhammad / by Hajjah Amina Adil ; retold by Karima Sperling and illustrated by Alia Sperling.
p. cm.
ISBN 1-930409-41-9
1. Muhammad, Prophet, d. 632--Biography--Juvenile literature. 2. Muslims--Saudi Arabia --Biography--Juvenile literature. I. Sperling, Karima. II. Sperling, Alia. III. Adil, Hajjah Amina. Muhammad, the messenger of Islam. IV. Title.
BP75.A345 2006
297.6'3--dc22
[B]

2006016256

Published and Distributed by:
Naqshbandi-Haqqani Sufi Order of America
17195 Silver Parkway, #201
Fenton, MI 48430 USA
Tel: (888) 278-6624
Fax: (810) 815-0518
Email: staff@naqshbandi.org
Web: www.naqshbandi.org

Dedication

We begin in the Name of Allah, the Most Merciful, the Most Compassionate. We pray He accept our humble efforts to honor His most beloved Prophet, Muhammad Mustafa ﷺ. We pray that He use this book to make His Truth and Love flower in the hearts of all children everywhere.

As with all our efforts this book was done for the honor and love of our Prophet, Muhammad Mustafa ﷺ, and for his representative, our master, Shaykh Muhammad Nazim al-Haqqani, and his khalif, Shaykh Muhammad Hisham Kabbani.

This book is being completed in the month of *Mawlid*, almost two years after the passing of Hajjah Amina Adil, may Allah sanctify her soul. She was a very special woman who is greatly missed. Since meeting her twenty five years ago she has served as a model of a wife, a mother and grandmother, a follower of the Prophet ﷺ and the shaykh, and a lover of God.

Hajjah Amina, called Hajjah Anna, or mother, by all who knew her, spent her life in service. She served Allah and His Prophet ﷺ and her husband, Shaykh Nazim Adil al-Haqqani, the Grand Shaykh of the Naqshbandi Tariqat. In serving them she found herself serving all of us as well; feeding us, listening to us, advising and teaching us.

She taught mostly by her example rather than by her words. When asked to speak she would usually tell stories. She was a treasure house of stories of the prophets and the saints. Women, children and men, if they were lucky, would gather around her to listen to her stories. These stories were like her old friends. She had heard them as a child. She had told them to her children and grandchildren. She had lived with them her entire life and she knew them intimately. In her last years she was unable to hold back the emotions these stories evoked in her, and she would have to pause often before going on. She

was still learning from them while passing their wisdom on to us. They lit up her life as she illuminated ours.

Her telling of the life of the Prophet Muhammad ﷺ is unique in our time. She had no need to make the Prophet ﷺ a modern man or even a human being at our level of understanding. She knew him as a cosmic figure whose reality is far beyond our limited understanding. What makes her telling so different is that she never forgets that Muhammad Rasulullah ﷺ is primarily a spiritual being of immense and incomparable capacity. This is evidenced by the fact that the Night Journey makes up almost a full third of the book. She does not shy away from miraculous events or wondrous tales. These stories, however you choose to understand them, figuratively or literally, add the depth and otherworldliness to the image of the Prophet ﷺ that he deserves and requires.

There are many books for children and adults that tell the story of the life of the Prophet ﷺ. Each brings its own view and shading to the picture of this most remarkable figure. Most, however, seem to find it more comfortable to portray the Prophet ﷺ as a very human figure, a sort of CEO of God's Great Company, a leader of men, a generous and courageous man who loved children and small animals. In Hajjah Anna's telling, the Prophet ﷺ is a spiritual figure of immense proportions, spanning the whole of creation. His nature encompasses all of us and everything else. With her wonderful sense of story telling she conveys the majesty and uniquely spiritual aspect of our great Prophet ﷺ.

Her original six hundred page book should be read by all. This small version is, I hope, perfect for children for whom the magical, the wondrous, and the spiritual are still an acceptable and believable part of everyday life. It is hoped that Hajjah Anna's book will foster love for Allah's Dearest Prophet ﷺ to grow in the hearts of our children and to serve, throughout their lives, as inspiration and consolation. It is also hoped that the light Hajjah Anna passed to us will continue to be shared.

This book is also dedicated to her daughter, Hajjah Naziha Kabbani, at whose request it was written. She is in her humble, gentle way, stepping into

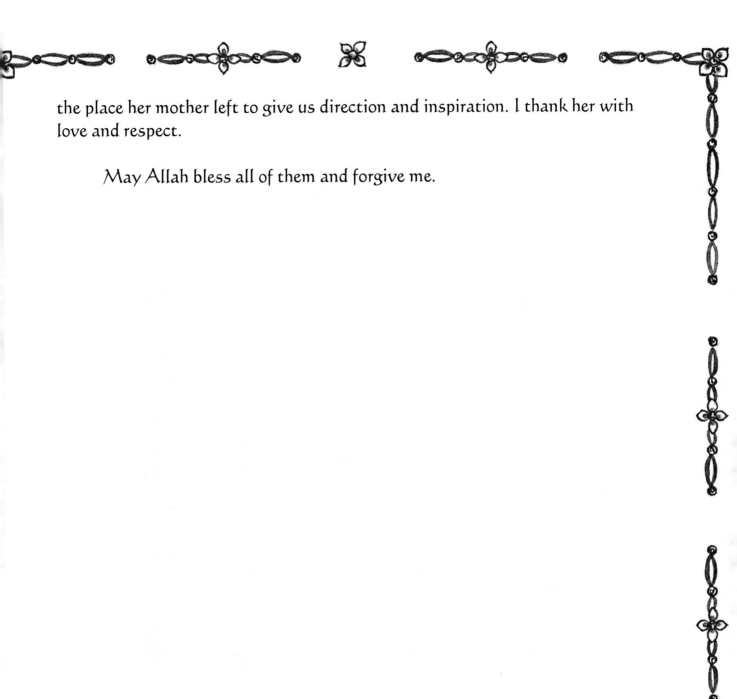

the place her mother left to give us direction and inspiration. I thank her with love and respect.

May Allah bless all of them and forgive me.

Acknowledgements

Thanks go always to Allah, Lord of the Worlds, for continuing in His Mercy to send us Guidance. All Light is His and to Him is our journey.

Thanks again and again to Radhia Shukrullah whose translation skill, insight and love channeled Hajjah Amina's words and spirit into beautiful English.

Thanks to my family: to Aminah for her typing and computer skills; to Alia for her wonderful drawings and for doing them so quickly, her light burning downstairs through many a dark night; to Munir for patience, support and very picky editing; and to Karam for turning a Word document into a book.

Thank you to Taher Siddiqui for coloring and designing the covers and for his patience and technical expertise.

Thank you to Mahmud and Aliya Shelton for in depth reading and advice on all levels. Thanks also to Sonia Shaykh for proofreading and child testing.

Table of Contents

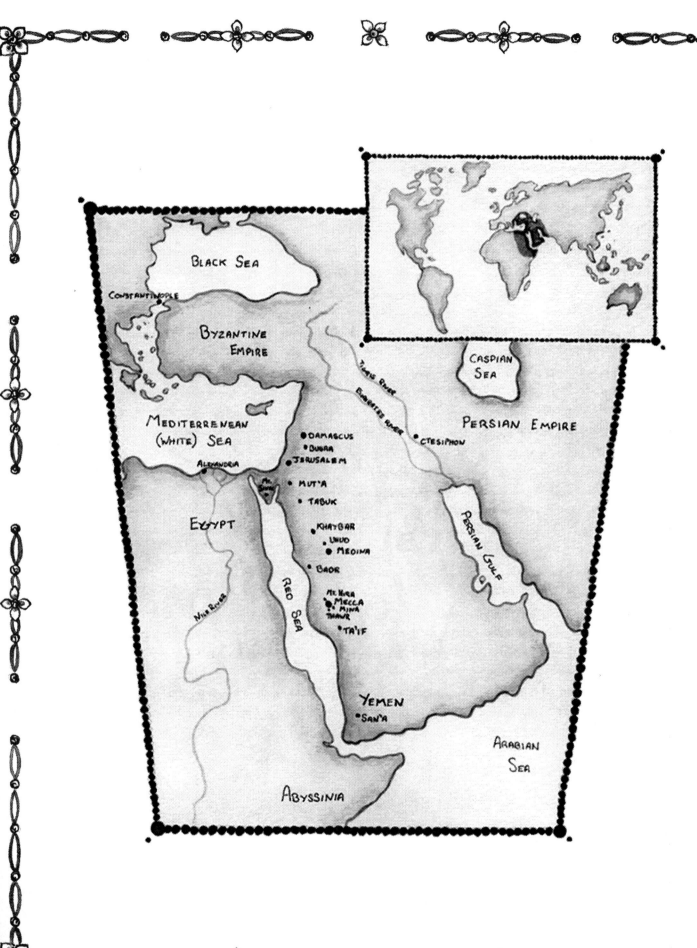

BLACK SEA

CONSTANTINOPLE

BYZANTINE EMPIRE

MEDITERRENEAN (WHITE) SEA

ALEXANDRA

EGYPT

CASPIAN SEA

PERSIAN EMPIRE

TIGRIS RIVER

EUPHRATES RIVER

CTESIPHON

DAMASCUS
BUSRA
JERUSALEM
MUT'A
TABUK
KHAYBAR
UHUD
MEDINA
BADR

PERSIAN GULF

RED SEA

NILE RIVER

Mt. Hira
MECCA
Mina
THAWR
TA'IF

YEMEN
SAN'A

ARABIAN SEA

ABYSSINIA

In The Beginning

Before there was earth or sea, before there was sky or stars, before there was the world as we know it, there was Allah and only Allah. There never was a time before He was or when He was not. He was never born and He was never created. He always was and He always will be, forever and ever without end. When the day arrives that His big, beautiful creation of stars and universes, people and *Jinn* ceases to be, Allah will remain Glorious, Magnificent and Radiant just as He always was. From Him we came and to Him we will return in our final homecoming. In reality there is nothing other, only Allah.

There came a time, however, very, very long ago, that Allah, Glorious and Mighty is He, decided to begin the creation of the world. He wanted this world to be like a mirror that would reflect His Perfect Beauty and Glory, so He made it from His own Radiant Light. The first thing He made was a smaller light that He called the light of Muhammad ﷺ. This light rested in the Presence of its Lord, light within Light, for as long as Allah willed it to rest, and it was for a very, very long time.

Then Allah divided this light of Muhammad ﷺ into four parts. Of the first part He made the *Qalam*, the Pen from whose tip the words of Allah flow, creating and designing the form of the world by the Will of its Lord. Of the second part He made the *Lawh ul-Mahfudh*, the Tablets on which the destiny of the world would be written and take shape. From the third part He made the *'Arsh*, the Throne which would be the seat of Power and Authority to keep

order in the world. These rested in the Presence of their Lord for as long as Allah willed, and it was for a very, very long time.

Then Allah commanded the Pen to write. The Pen, because it is a living thing and has a voice, said: "Oh my Lord, what shall I write?" "Write," it was commanded, "*Bismillahir Rahmanir Rahim.*"
And so the world was begun in the Name of Allah, the Kind and the Caring One.

Then Allah divided the remaining fourth part again into four parts and of these He made the Angelic worlds. Of the first part He made the angels who carry the *'Arsh*. Of the second part He made the Highest Heavens and the *Kursi*, the platform that rises up to the Throne. Of the third part He made the rest of the angelic company in all their different and wonderful variety. And they rested in the Presence of their Lord for as long as Allah willed, and it was for a very, very long time.

The fourth part He again divided into four parts, and of these He made the universe. Of the first part He made the skies. Of the second part He made the Earths. Of the third part He made the fire and the *Jinn*. And they rested in the Presence of their Lord for as long as Allah willed, and it was for a very, very long time.

The fourth part He again divided into four parts, and of these He made humankind. Of the first part He made the light on the faces of believers. Of the second part He made the light in the hearts of believers. Of the third part He made the light on the tongues of believers. And these lights rested in the Presence of their Lord for as long as Allah willed, and it was for a very, very long time.

From the fourth part Allah then made the soul of the Prophet Muhammad ﷺ looking just as his body would come to look except it was made out of light. Allah placed this precious soul in a lamp of green emerald and hung it from the Tree of Certainty in the Highest Heaven, where it glowed and sparkled. This soul began to make *dhikr*, praising and celebrating the many wondrous acts of its Lord that it had witnessed. And it continued making *dhikr* in the Presence of its Lord for as long as Allah willed, and it was for a very, very long time.

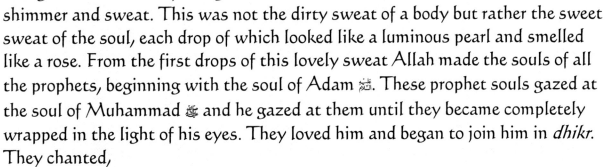

As this soul of Muhammad ﷺ, made from the light of Muhammad ﷺ, thought about its Lord, it began to shimmer and sweat. This was not the dirty sweat of a body but rather the sweet sweat of the soul, each drop of which looked like a luminous pearl and smelled like a rose. From the first drops of this lovely sweat Allah made the souls of all the prophets, beginning with the soul of Adam ﷺ. These prophet souls gazed at the soul of Muhammad ﷺ and he gazed at them until they became completely wrapped in the light of his eyes. They loved him and began to join him in *dhikr*. They chanted,

La ilaha ill'Allah, Muhammadur Rasulullah.

"There is one God, Allah, and Muhammad ﷺ is His Messenger." And they made *dhikr* in the Presence of their Lord for as long as Allah willed, and it was for a very, very long time.

Allah continued to create the world from the drops of luminous sweat that fell from the soul of the Prophet Muhammad ﷺ in the lamp on the tree in the Highest Heaven. From the sweat on his head Allah made the souls of the angels. From the sweat on his face Allah made the sun, the moon, and the stars. From the sweat on his chest Allah made the souls of the shaykhs and the martyrs. From the sweat on his back Allah made the *Bayt ul-Ma'mur* in Heaven, the Ka'aba in Mecca, and the *Bayt ul-Maqdis* in Jerusalem. From the

sweat of his eyebrows Allah made the souls of all the believing people. From the sweat of his feet Allah made the pastures, forests and seas from east to west.

Now all these souls gathered around the blessed soul of the Prophet Muhammad ﷺ glowing in the lamp of green emerald on the Tree of Certainty in the Highest Heaven. They gazed at him and he gazed at them until they became wrapped in the light of his eyes for as long as Allah willed, and it was for a very, very long time.

Those souls who looked at his head would become kings or heads of state when they came to be born into this world. Those who looked at his eyes would memorize the Quran. Those who looked at his eyebrows would be artists. Those who looked at his cheeks would be doers of good. Those who looked at his mouth would be judges, and those who looked at his teeth would be great beauties. Those who looked at his beard would be warriors. Those who looked at his upper arms would be archers, and those who looked at his neck, merchants. Those who looked at his palms would be generous. Those who looked at his chest would be learned. Those who looked at his back would be humble, at his stomach would be contented, at his knees would pray much and at his feet would wander the world.

Those who looked but saw nothing would believe in nothing, and those souls who refused to look at all would become cruel and tyrannical.

Then all these souls of all the unborn people of the Earth lined up in four rows. In the first row stood the prophets, then the saints, then the believers, and behind them in the last row stood the unbelievers. And we remained in the glow of the light of Muhammad ﷺ, within the Light of Allah for as long as Allah willed us to remain, and it was for a very, very long time.

Allah created our world in beauty, with its deep seas, rushing rivers and calm lakes, with its snow covered mountains, sandy beaches and green valleys. He made it beautiful and useful, as only He could envision it. Then He made creatures to live on it. He made the elegant horse and the scaly iguana, the soaring eagle and the tiny snail. He made all of them as only He could envision them.

Then He wanted a deputy to be His representative in this world to know its value and take care of it. Allah took dirt from the four corners of the Earth and mixed it with water from the four rivers of Paradise to make clay. From this clay of many colors He formed a beautiful body and into it He breathed the soul of the Prophet Adam 🕌, which He had made a long, long time before. From Adam 🕌 He made Adam's 🕌 wife, Hawa 🕌. Within them He put the seeds of all the people who would eventually be born and grow on Earth and whose souls already waited making *dhikr* in Heaven.

Allah, Generous and Kind, also gave to our father Adam 🕌 another portion of the light of Muhammad 🕌. This shone like a lamp from Adam's 🕌 forehead, lighting the way and guiding those around him to the straight path. Allah cautioned Adam 🕌 and Hawa 🕌 to protect this light by being righteous and kind, for it would pass from them to those of their children who were worthy.

And so it happened. Adam 🕌 and Hawa 🕌 had many children who went on to have their own children until the beautiful Earth was completely peopled. But only one of their sons, Seth 🕌, carried the light of Muhammad 🕌 on his forehead. This light was then passed from believing parent to believing child, from loving parent to loving child, down through the ages until it would come to alight on the one to whom it belonged, the Prophet Muhammad 🕌.

From Seth 🕌 the light passed to Idris 🕌, and from him to Nuh 🕌, and then to Hud 🕌, and on to Salih 🕌. The light shone from the Prophet Ibrahim 🕌 and his nephew, Lut 🕌, and passed on to Ismail 🕌 and Ishaq 🕌. It glowed from Ya'qub 🕌 and then from his son, Yusuf 🕌. It passed from Ayyub 🕌 to Dhul Kifl 🕌 and then to Shu'ayb 🕌. It streamed from Musa 🕌 and his brother, Harun 🕌. It passed on to Yusha 🕌 and to Samuel 🕌. It radiated around Da'ud 🕌 and his

son, Sulaiman ﷺ. To Ilyas ﷺ it passed and to Alyas'a ﷺ, to Yunus ﷺ and then to Sha'ya ﷺ. It shone from Armiya ﷺ, Daniel ﷺ and Dhul Qarnain ﷺ. It passed on to Zakariya ﷺ and his son, Yahya ﷺ, and glowed like a halo around the Prophet 'Isa ﷺ. Finally, the fortunate day dawned on which it alighted on the forehead of Allah's beloved, the Last Prophet, Muhammad Mustafa ﷺ.

2

The Parents of the Prophet ﷺ

Surrounded by the vast hot sands of Arabia is an outcrop of jagged, rocky peaks hiding sandy valleys in which people have been living for centuries. In this remote place the Prophet Ibrahim ﷺ left his Egyptian wife, Hajar ﷺ, and their little son, Ismail ﷺ. This is where the spring of *Zam Zam* miraculously bubbled out of the ground to quench Ismail's ﷺ desperate thirst. This is where Ibrahim ﷺ had been commanded to sacrifice his beloved son. This is where Ibrahim ﷺ and his son, Ismail ﷺ, had rebuilt the ancient house of worship known as the Ka'aba and established the rites of pilgrimage.

By the sixth century (CE) a small city had grown up in this protected place. It was called Mecca and the people who lived there were descendants of the Prophet Ismail ﷺ and were known as Quraysh. They had forgotten about the sacred well of *Zam Zam* and it had been buried under a mountain of sand. They had also forgotten the teachings of Ibrahim ﷺ and Ismail ﷺ. The light that they carried had been buried under a mountain of ignorance. Into this darkness a great light was waiting to descend, and there were signs that began to appear to let the people of Mecca know that something very special was about to take place.

One of the nobles of Mecca was named Abdul Muttalib and he had a dream. He dreamed that he was shown the place of the sacred spring of *Zam Zam*. When he woke in the morning he determined to dig away the sand and dirt and re-open the sacred well. But he could find no one to believe him or to help him.

So he went to the Ka'aba and asked Allah to give him ten sons who would grow strong and help him in his task of finding and securing *Zam Zam*. Abdul Muttalib promised that if Allah gave him ten sons he would sacrifice one of them on the doorstep of the Ka'aba in the name of the Almighty Lord as a way of saying thank you. This was a custom of the people of those times who no longer understood the worship of Allah according to His Prophets and His Books.

Abdul Muttalib married several wives and they began to have children. During this time Abdul Muttalib had another dream. In his sleep he saw a tree begin to grow out of his back. This tree had four branches: one growing up to the sky, one growing down into the ground, one growing to the East and one to the West. It was a tree on which every kind of fruit found anywhere in the world were all growing together. It was a tree of incredible beauty, and Abdul Muttalib saw the people of the whole world coming together to pay their respect to that tree. Among those people he saw his family of Quraysh. Some of them hugged one of the branches of the tree while the others tried to chop it down. Then Abdul Muttalib saw in his dream the most beautiful man glowing with light and at the foot of the tree he saw two grandfatherly shaykhs.

In those days dreams were taken very seriously because without prophets or books, dreams were the clearest way of hearing Allah's wishes. Abdul Muttalib went immediately to see a man who had the ability to help people understand their dreams. This man told Abdul Muttalib that a prophet was coming and would be born among his grandchildren. This prophet would visit the Highest Heavens, yet would die and be buried in the ground. He would

capture the hearts of all from East to West. Half of the Quraysh would accept him and half would fight him.

The beautiful man in the dream was the religion that this prophet would bring. The two shaykhs were the Prophets Nuh and Ibrahim. The coming prophet would have enemies who would be destroyed like those of Nuh were destroyed in the flood, and he and his followers would belong to the nation of Ibrahim.

Allah did give Abdul Muttalib many children, including ten fine healthy sons who grew to manhood. And Abdul Muttalib set about keeping his promise. He and his sons began digging in the spot he had seen in his first dream. After much hard labor they uncovered the well of *Zam Zam*. They also found two deer-shaped ornaments made

of red gold buried there since the time of Ismail and one hundred swords and one hundred coats of armor from the time of the Prophet Da'ud. The weapons they melted down to make doors for the Ka'aba and the ornaments they melted into golden decorations for those doors.

Now the rest of his promise must be kept. Abdul Muttalib must sacrifice one of his beloved sons. They drew lots and Abdullah's name was chosen.

Abdullah was the youngest of Abdul Muttalib's sons, the most handsome and the one from whom the light of Muhammad shone clearly. The family was heartbroken. But a man of honor must keep his word and so, like the Prophet Ibrahim, Abdul Muttalib began to ready himself for the ultimate sacrifice. Before the deed could be done a wise old man suggested that lots be drawn again but this time between Abdullah and ten fine camels. The lot fell

again on Abdullah ﷺ. They increased the numbers of camels, to twenty, then thirty, and still the lot fell on Abdullah ﷺ. It was only when they offered to sacrifice one hundred camels did the choice fall on the camels rather than Abdullah ﷺ. This is why the payment for the death of a man is equal to one hundred camels. Abdul Muttalib had kept his promise and Abdullah ﷺ lived.

Abdullah ﷺ then began to experience strange things. He saw light spreading out before and around him. The ground greeted him when he sat upon it and the dead trees became alive when he leaned his back against their trunks. He had dreams very much like the one his father had had of a tree of light growing from his back whose branches stretched to the four corners of the world.

The people of Mecca were impressed by the light shining from Abdullah ﷺ and they wanted it for their own. They began to offer their daughters to him in marriage in the hope that their grandchildren would be carriers of this light.

But Abdul Muttalib was a wise man and he knew that he had a duty to protect this light. He began searching for a wife for Abdullah ﷺ. He was not looking for a princess, although there were some that were asking. He was not looking for a daughter of a powerful or wealthy family, although there were many of those asking. He was looking for a girl whose heart was pure and filled with belief. He found her in the small oasis of Yathrib, that later became known as Medina, six days journey north of Mecca. She was of a noble family, but neither rich nor powerful. Her beauty and sweetness were well known throughout the whole region. Her father had refused all the young men who had asked to marry her. Her name was Aminah ﷺ, daughter of Wahb.

Wahb could see that Abdullah ﷺ was a fine young man of the best family. He could also see the light that Abdullah ﷺ carried and he immediately agreed to the marriage. Aminah ﷺ, although shy, also accepted and the contract was drawn up that very day. The marriage itself followed quickly.

Abdullah ﷺ and Aminah ﷺ became man and wife on the night before the first *Juma'a,* Friday eve, in the month of *Rajab.* This night we call *Lailat ul-Raghaib,* the Night of Desires. It was on this night that the pure elements that would make up the body of the Prophet Muhammad ﷺ descended into the womb of Aminah ﷺ as a pearl would form in the shell of the sea.

At this time Allah commanded the guardians of Paradise to open wide the gates. Messenger angels were sent to all the souls living in the Heavens and on the Earth that the light they had been waiting for, the light they had loved since their creation, was being unveiled. Part of the light-filled soul of Muhammad ﷺ was leaving the green lamp on the Tree of Certainty and entering the lower world. His time had arrived. The messenger angels told all those in the spirit kingdoms and those whose hearts were open in the earthly kingdoms to prepare feasts, light incense and invite their neighbors to share in the joy. They gathered and sang the praises of Allah Almighty and His beloved Muhammad Mustafa ﷺ in all the languages and voices the world has to offer. Even today we continue to honor this tradition by celebrating the first Friday eve in *Rajab* every year.

That night the birds and beasts of the entire world rejoiced together without fear of each other. The animals living in the area of Mecca spoke in human language that night and they said, "By the Lord of the Ka'aba the light of the world is coming." The whole Earth shook in joy and all the statues of false gods that were worshipped by the ignorant people fell on their faces and shattered into tiny pieces.

Wise men knew that at long last the awaited prophet was coming to deliver Allah's final message for the people of the whole world.

3

The Year of The Elephant

The year of the Prophet's ﷺ birth was remembered by the people of Mecca for another reason as well. It was called the Year of the Elephant. A powerful king of Yemen, named Abraha, had built a huge and richly decorated church. His intention was to attract people to make pilgrimage there and bring their money and their trade with them. This would make his city an important center. When the pilgrims continued going to the Ka'aba and not to his city he gathered an enormous army, with foot soldiers, and camels, and warhorses. He intended to destroy the Ka'aba completely so that his church would have no rival.

Abraha's army marched out of Yemen led by a mighty elephant decked out for war, whose name was Mahmud. It set out across the desert of Arabia until it came within sight of Mecca. At this point the great war-elephant, Mahmud, obedient only to Allah, sat down and refused to budge. They prodded and poked him. They offered him treats. They beat him with sharp hooks. But Mahmud remained true to Allah's command. The other animals were used to following the lead of Mahmud, and so the whole army stopped dead in its tracks.

Meanwhile the Quraysh wondered what they should do to defend their city. Abdul Muttalib advised them that the Ka'aba was not theirs to protect. They were a small force against Abraha's mighty army. If they fought, many

would die. Instead, they should leave Allah Almighty to protect His Holy House. Abdul Muttalib ordered all the men, women and children of Quraysh to leave their houses and sacred mosque to the protection of their Lord and run to hide in the craggy hills above the city.

From this vantage point they watched as Mahmud the elephant lay down and the whole army came to a stop just outside the gates of the city. Then they saw a large flock of heavenly birds, called *ababil* in Arabic, flying in from the sea. Each bird held in its small beak a stone the size of a lentil, and in each small claw it held another. They flew over the city of Mecca and over the heads of the Quraysh watching in the mountains. They flew until they hovered over the army of Abraha. By the command of Allah, a wind rose up from Hell and baked these stones until they were red-hot and glowing.

The *ababil* pelted the army of Abraha with their stones. Some soldiers were hit and died right away while others managed to escape but later sickened and died. Each soldier ran in a different direction. Abraha himself was hit and later died. Abraha's mighty army, by Allah's command, was defeated by the heavenly birds and the obedience of the elephant.

Abdul Muttalib victoriously led his people back in safety to their homes. The Quraysh felt even more respect for the wisdom of their leader, Abdul Muttalib. They also began to be aware of just how holy their Ka'aba must be and just how real was the protection and presence of its unseen Lord, Allah Almighty.

At this time Aminah ؏ was pregnant, and the light that had shone from Abdullah ؏ passed to the baby in her womb and shone all around her. She began to see and experience wonderful things.

Early in her first month she awoke to find a serene and shining man in her room. He looked at her calmly and addressed the baby inside of her: *"As-salamu alaykum, ya Muhammad ؕ. Peace be upon you, O Muhammad ؕ."* Aminah ؏ was startled and asked, "Who are you?" "I am the father of all mankind," he answered. "I am

Adam 🕊, and I, who am called God's deputy on Earth, have come to greet the best of all my children, the Prince of the Worlds."

In her second month, Aminah 🕊 awoke to the presence of another man of light in her room. He greeted her baby with the words, "*As-salamu alaykum*, O child for whom the whole creation is longing." He told her he was the Prophet Seth 🕊, meaning gift of God, because his parents had longed for him for many, many years.

In her third month Aminah 🕊 had another visitor. He said, "*As-salamu alaykum*, O blessed one wrapped in the robes of mercy." He was the Prophet Idris 🕊, who is tailor to the people of Paradise.

In her fourth month a dark-skinned visitor woke Aminah 🕊 saying, "*As-salamu alaykum*, O one chosen above all others.*" This was the Prophet Nuh 🕊, who was chosen to survive the flood and from whose children we all descend.

In the fifth month the Prophet Hood 🕊 visited her. He was the last in his line of prophets and he greeted her baby with, "*As-salamu alaykum*, O last and perfect one in the whole chain of prophets."

In the sixth month the Prophet Ibrahim 🕊, who is himself called the dear friend of Allah, came, looking dignified and kindly. He greeted her baby with, "*As-salamu alaykum*, O most beloved of Allah."

In her seventh month Aminah 🕊 had a gentle visitor of light. He was Ismail 🕊, the obedient son and trusted companion of Ibrahim 🕊. He greeted the baby with, "*As-salamu alaykum*, O true friend of Allah."

In her eighth month Aminah 🕊 awoke to see a tall man of friendly expression. He greeted her baby with, "*As-salamu alaykum*, O mighty prophet

of Allah." He told her he was Musa ﷺ, who had freed his people from the grip of Pharaoh.

In the ninth month a man of light entered Aminah's ﵟ room dressed in what appeared to be wool. He said, "*As-salamu alaykum*, O Messenger of Allah." He told her he was 'Isa ﷺ, who was called the Word of Allah. He told her that her time had come. The birth was near. She must get herself ready.

During her whole pregnancy Aminah ﵟ said she never felt sick or tired like other pregnant women. From her body came a sweet scent of heavenly perfume and she always heard a soft voice within her womb praising God. In her sixth month she was told to name her baby Muhammad, meaning the one deserving praise, and that he was mentioned in the Bible as Ahmad. Angels surrounded and protected her at all times while she carried her baby.

But the situation was very different for his father, Abdullah ﵞ. When Abdullah ﵞ learned he was to be a father he knew he must also prepare. He needed to support and feed his new family. Abdul Muttalib suggested that Abdullah ﵞ make a journey to the oasis of Yathrib, Medina, the home of Aminah's ﵟ family. There he could collect his family's share of dates and bring them back to feed his family with some and sell the rest.

Abdullah ﵞ set off. He gathered the dates and on his return, just outside the city, he became ill. He died and was buried. All the angels cried for Aminah ﵟ, left without her dear husband, and for the baby who, even before he was born, was orphaned. The angels even went so far as to question Allah. "How could you send your beloved Muhammad ﷺ into that cruel world as a weak and fatherless orphan?" they asked. Allah answered them: "It is true that a child needs a father for protection in the world and for training and teaching, but My

beloved has no need of anyone but Me. I will teach him. I will protect him. I will train him. Other children cry out for their father when they are hurt or in need, but My beloved Muhammad ﷺ will call out only for Me and I will answer him. He has no need of anyone but Me."

The Birth of the Prophet ﷺ

Aminah ؓ was in her ninth month and ready to give birth. It was in the early hours of a Monday morning, the twelfth of the month of *Rabi' ul-Awwal*, and still quite dark. She was all alone. Suddenly there was a great noise and she began to feel afraid. A white bird flew in and sat itself softly on her chest. Her fear left her. A cool drink was mysteriously handed to her and her heart filled with peace and joy.

A group of tall, beautiful women appeared to her and gathered in a protective circle around her. One of the ladies spoke saying, "I am Hawa, wife of the Prophet Adam ﷺ." Then each of the ladies introduced herself. One was Sarah ؓ, wife of the Prophet Ibrahim ﷺ and mother of the Prophet Ishaq ﷺ. One was Buhayyid ؓ, the mother of Musa ﷺ. Another was Asiya ؓ, the wife of Pharaoh in the time of Musa ﷺ. One was Maryam ؓ, the mother of the Prophet 'Isa ﷺ. The others were ladies of Paradise. They had come to help and to welcome the Holy Prophet ﷺ into this world. They encircled her and their robes formed a curtain from the eyes of the world. The noises she had first heard kept getting louder. She saw a white shape like a curtain being drawn across the sky that veiled her from the prying eyes of *Jinn*. Then a flock of birds with beaks of green emerald and wings of red ruby flew down. They fluttered all around her so that she could feel the soft beating of their wings on her skin.

They flew around her in circles.

She said that then Allah removed the veil from her eyes and from her bed in Mecca she could see the whole world from East to West. She saw three banners come down from the Heavens. One was placed in the East, one in the West and one on the very top of the Ka'aba. Men of light came from the heavens carrying golden bowls covered with precious jewels and they helped the ladies in delivering the baby so that Aminah felt no hardship or pain.

When she looked again the child was already born. He was wrapped in a piece of white silk and he was already circumcised. The air around her glowed with a bright light. The baby bent his little head to the ground in *sajda* and then lifted his right forefinger. She leaned over him and heard him say softly:

Ash-hadu an la ilaha ill'Allah
Wa inni Rasulullah
Allahu Akbar kabiran
Wal hamdulillahi kathiran
Wa subhanallahi bukratan wa asilan
Allahumma, ummati, ummati.

"I witness that there is no god but Allah and I am His messenger. Allah is the Greatest and Infinite Praise is due to Him. Glory to Allah in the morning and the evening. Please Allah, watch over my community."

The Blessed Prophet ﷺ began his life on this earth with prayer. The first thing he did was to bow his tiny head in humbleness to the Lord Almighty. The second thing he did was to ask for the safety and well being of his followers. From the moment of his birth he cared about and prayed for us. Though he was chosen above all others, this noble and generous soul, even in its weakest moment as a tiny helpless baby, praised Allah and prayed for us.

Aminah looked up and saw a white cloud out of which came the sounds of galloping horses. The cloud arrived and then  enveloped the newborn baby. A voice called out to her: "We are taking the baby to show him the whole world from the depths of the oceans to the heights of the mountains, and all the creatures that live upon it." In a few minutes the cloud

returned and the baby Muhammad ﷺ was handed back to his mother, wrapped now in a piece of green silk. A lovely smell of musk came from his tiny head.

Three angelic beings gathered around him. The first washed him seven times from a silver pitcher. The second took a dazzling ring from inside some wrappings of silk and pressed its surface against his tiny back between his shoulders until it left a mark in the shape of a circle with a point on top. The third took the baby and held him under his wing for a whole hour whispering secrets into his ear. Then they handed him back to his mother.

Outside Aminah's ﷺ small house the arrival of Muhammad ﷺ did not go unnoticed. After an unusually moist, cool night the sun rose on that day brighter than anyone could remember seeing it. The animals in all the world rejoiced and behaved as if they were tame. There was a fish that lived in the sea named *Zalmusa*. This fish had seventy heads and seventy tails, and a single scale on his mighty back could carry seventy small mountains. The morning the blessed Prophet ﷺ was born this fish was so deliriously happy that he flipped and flopped in joy deep in his ocean home. This made the seven seas to heave and roll, and there was not a creature within its depths that did not hear of the birth of the Prophet Muhammad ﷺ

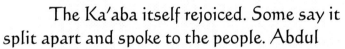

The Ka'aba itself rejoiced. Some say it split apart and spoke to the people. Abdul Muttalib was at the Ka'aba for morning prayers. He saw it shake and tremble and all the stone statues within it, which were worshipped by ignorant people, tottered and fell from their bases. And the Ka'aba, which has no windows, glowed as the many heavenly beings gathered inside with lights to celebrate the birth of the Prophet Muhammad ﷺ.

Abdul Muttalib quickly went to Aminah's ﷺ house to see if the baby had been born. He held him in his arms and breathed in the beautiful scent of musk that came from his sweet body. This perfume was so great that it wafted out of

Aminah's 🌸 house and blew through the streets of the city of Mecca, waking people from their sleep wondering what had happened. Even Abu Lahab, the Prophet's uncle, who was to be such an enemy to him later in life, woke with joy. He sent Thauba, his servant, to help Aminah 🌸. Aminah 🌸 nursed her baby for seven days and then Thauba nursed him.

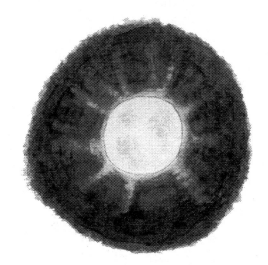

The light that had shone from Abdullah 🌸 and then passed to Aminah 🌸 now shone like a star from the forehead of the baby Muhammad ﷺ. His face looked like the full moon.

People living in far away places experienced miraculous things. To all who saw it, it was like *Laylat ul-Qadr*, the Night of Power. A king of Persia in the East saw a dream in which the end of his empire was foreshadowed and the coming of the Holy Prophet ﷺ foretold. A king in the far West saw the great light. His daughter who had been sick from childhood saw the light and was healed. This king and his family left their kingdom, their palaces and their treasures in search of the one to whom this light belonged. By the Will of Allah they arrived in Mecca within a few days. The king stood outside the small house of Aminah 🌸 and pleaded with her to allow them to see the baby.

Finally, she agreed to let these strangers peak at her newborn son. She gently opened the blankets and the light from his face shone to the heavens. For one hour the king and his family gazed at the baby. They kissed his hands and his feet. Then she covered the baby again and told the king he must leave. But the king could not leave that beautiful baby and begged to be allowed to see him just once more. Aminah 🌸 gave in. The king bent to kiss the tiny feet and his heart, blazing with the fire of his love, gave out and he was carried straight to Paradise.

The whole world, every rock, every tree, every animal in its own way celebrated the birth of its Prophet ﷺ. We continue to honor the month of his

birth with feasts and gifts and acts of kindness and charity. We recite the Quran and Dalail Khayrat. We read the stories of his life and remember him. We thank Allah for sending us such a kind and noble Prophet ﷺ to be our guide and our example.

As we pray that Allah bless our Prophet Muhammad ﷺ and raise him always higher and closer, and increase him in knowledge and beauty, we remember that he is still also praying for us. He began as a newborn baby and continues until today to turn his kind face towards us and beg Allah to forgive us for all the bad things we have done and all the good things we have left undone.

5

The Childhood of the Prophet ﷺ

In the year before the Holy Prophet's ﷺ birth little rain had fallen. Arabia is not just a dry sandy place. Whenever it rains grasses grow, and in most years there is some rain. But that year no rain came and the grasses dried up, so there was little to feed the goats and camels. This meant fewer baby animals were born and there was less milk and meat for the people of the desert, the Bedouin. They were both hungry and tired from walking long distances looking for pasture for their animals.

At the time of the birth of the Prophet ﷺ, however, rain began to fall. It was unusual for it to rain that late in the year but the pastures became green and the drought ended. This year was remembered as the "Year of the Solving of Difficulties." Because the rain fell the grasses grew, the goats and sheep ate and so did the people. In honor of the Prophet's ﷺ birth Allah continues to give special blessing to the water which falls as rain in the month of April of every year. We collect a little of this rain if we can and drink it for healing and remembrance.

Mecca was a dry dusty city built in the valleys between rocky mountains. It depended on trade for its food. It had no gardens nor date palms and nothing much with which to feed animals. The Bedouin were people who lived outside the city. They pastured goats, sheep and camels in the hills and valleys of

Arabia. The Bedouin moved with their flocks from one pasture to another. They lived a healthy, outdoor life. Their children drank a lot of rich goat and camel milk and ate fresh meat. They grew strong and healthy. The desert was a better place to raise young children than the city.

It was the custom among the noble Qurayshi mothers to give their babies to Bedouin women to care for. Every year the Bedouin women who had nursing babies of their own would come to Mecca to find another baby to nurse. The Qurayshi mothers would pay them to care for their babies for a few years. Even though it must have been heartbreaking to part with their little babies the mothers wanted what was best for them. After they had grown strong the Bedouin women returned the children to their own mothers in Mecca. This way the Qurayshi children got a good healthy start in life and the Bedouin families made some extra money to buy clothes and other things they needed for their own children.

In the year of the Holy Prophet's ﷺ birth, because of the drought, the Bedouin women were particularly anxious to foster the babies of the wealthy Qurayshi women. The mothers of the tribe of Sa'ad loaded their babies on

donkeys and set out for the city. One of them, Halima as-Sa'adia ؓ, was having particular difficulty. Her donkey was weak and thin from not having enough to eat. Halima ؓ herself was weak for the same reason. She could barely hold her baby and stay on the slowly moving donkey. But the pastures were greening up and things were getting better and she knew she would be able to feed another nursing baby.

She fell behind her friends because her donkey was so tired and slow. When she finally reached Mecca all her friends had found babies to care for. She asked if there was one left for her to take. They told her that one baby boy remained. No one wanted him because his father had died and they feared there was no one to pay a foster mother.

Halima ؓ did not want to go home empty handed, so she searched out the small house of Aminah ؓ. Her heart melted when she saw the beautiful baby boy. His face was so bright and sweet. She loved him right away and determined to take him even if they could not pay her. But Abdul Muttalib took good care of his grandson and offered to pay Halima ۴ well for her service.

Halima ۴ put her own little daughter down and began to nurse Aminah's ۴ baby, Muhammad ﷺ. He would only drink from her right side. When she offered the left breast the little baby raised his eyebrows as if to say, "That belongs to my foster sister. Only one side belongs to me." Halima ۴ was amazed, and her heart ached for this fatherless baby who thought only of others.

It was in this way that Halima as-Sa'adia ۴ went home on her little donkey, carrying in her fortunate arms the light of the worlds, Muhammad ﷺ. Later she said that from that moment on everything in her life got better. Her donkey, which had been hardly able to walk, now trotted quickly along with strength and energy. She caught up to her friends who had left quite a while before her. She felt stronger also, and her milk became plentiful. She later said that her donkey had become as strong as a mule and she herself had become as strong as a lioness.

When she reached home, Halima ۴ put Muhammad ﷺ in a wooden cradle and tied it out of harms way in the branches of a tree. A neighbor of hers, Umm Habiba, who was old and blind, came to visit and hear the news of the city. She was overcome by a wonderful smell and could not believe that Halima ۴ had enough money to buy such expensive perfume. But Halima ۴ told her it was not perfume. It was the scent that came naturally from the body of the tiny Qurayshi baby she had brought back with her. Umm Habiba bent her head over the cradle to better smell the wonderful perfume. The baby reached up his small hands and stroked her blind eyes and suddenly Umm Habiba could see again.

So many wonderful things happened to Halima 🌸 while Muhammad ﷺ was with her. She began to love him even more than her own children. He grew into a strong little boy. The first words that he spoke were:

La ilaha ill'Allah, wahdahu, la sharika lak. Lahul mulk,
wa lahul hamd, wa huwa 'ala kulli shay'in qadir.

"There is no God but Allah. He is One, without partners. His is the kingdom and to Him all praise is due, and He has power over all things."

During his stay in the desert Muhammad ﷺ would help his foster brothers and sisters take care of the goats and sheep. They would take them out in the morning to eat the fresh grass and bring them home at dark for safety. The Prophet ﷺ later said that all the prophets at one time in their lives were shepherds. Wherever Muhammad ﷺ led the goats the grass became greener. The trees bowed down before him and the rocks under his feet whispered their greetings.

One day, however, something very unusual happened. A lion came out of the hills. The other children ran to hide but Muhammad ﷺ held his ground. His brothers thought for sure he would be eaten, but instead they saw the lion lie down at his feet and begin to lick them. Muhammad ﷺ stroked the fierce lion's head as if he were a kitten.

Then out of the sky came a huge white bird. It swooped down and picked up little Muhammad ﷺ and carried him to the top of a large rock nearby. The children screamed for their parents who came running as fast as they could. They found Muhammad ﷺ unhurt on top of the rock.

It had not been a bird but the Archangel Jibra'il 🌸 who had picked him up. Jibra'il 🌸 had cut open the boy's chest and taken out his heart and washed it in a silver bowl. Much later Muhammad ﷺ explained that in each heart is a bit of fear. This fear is like an invitation to Shaytan. When Shaytan whispers it is this fear that listens. The heart of the Holy Prophet ﷺ was washed clean of fear so that Shaytan would never have any power over him.

Then the Angel put his heart back in his chest and sewed it up with a silken thread. The stitches were still visible when the terrified foster parents arrived. Halima ﷺ knew that if something happened to the boy while in her care she would never forgive herself. Quickly she got him ready and, mounted on her little donkey, she brought Muhammad ﷺ back to Mecca and to his family.

In this way Muhammad ﷺ, at about four or five years of age, came back to live with his mother, Aminah ﷺ. She was very happy to have her son with her again. But Allah did not give them much time together. In a couple of years Aminah ﷺ died and the Prophet ﷺ went to live in the house of his beloved grandfather, Abdul Muttalib.

Abdul Muttalib was an old man by now. Only four of his ten sons remained alive. All day he would sit on a carpet in the shade of the Ka'aba helping people settle their disagreements and finding solutions for those in trouble. He allowed none of his many grandchildren to sit there with him. They disrupted the serious talk of the men. Only little Muhammad ﷺ was allowed to

sit beside his grandfather because he was unusually quiet and respectful. He listened seriously to the talk of the grown-ups, sometimes asking helpful questions. Abdul Muttalib loved having Muhammad ﷺ near him and would send for him if he were out playing. Muhammad ﷺ grew up in the shade of the blessed Ka'aba.

Then Abdul Muttalib got sick and died. Muhammad ﷺ had been orphaned three times before the age of eight. On his deathbed Abdul Muttalib spoke to his four remaining sons. Hamza ﷺ and Abbas ﷺ were still young and unmarried. Abu Lahab had a large family of his own. So Abdul Muttalib asked his son, Abu Talib, to take Muhammad ﷺ into his home and raise him as a son. He told Abu Talib to watch over Muhammad ﷺ with care and to do nothing to undermine his noble nature.

Abu Talib respected his father's wishes. He took great care of his nephew, Muhammad ﷺ, and raised him with love and kindness. Although he never publicly became Muslim, Abu Talib did everything in his power throughout his life to protect Muhammad ﷺ and to help him.

Abu Talib was a merchant. He traveled to distant places to sell and trade. When Muhammad ﷺ was nine or ten he accompanied his uncle on such a

 journey to help take care of the camels that carried the trade goods. They were going to Syria. It was summer and very hot in the desert of Arabia. The camels walked slowly in the heat. The men of the caravan began to

notice that a little white cloud seemed to float at all times at the end of the long line of camels where the young Muhammad ﷺ walked. The cloud gave him some shelter from the scorching sun.

A Christian monk living in the hills above the town of Busra looked out over the desert and saw the caravan approaching. He saw the fluffy white cloud following it. His name was Buhayra ؈ and he had studied the Bible for many, many years. He knew this was a sign that Allah's Beloved, the Prophet ﷺ he had read about in the Holy Books, had finally come. When the caravan stopped to rest Buhayra ؈ came down from his cave and went among the people looking for the one he had been waiting for.

He saw the light shining from the face of the young camel boy and he asked about him. Abu Talib said that this was his son but Buhayra ؈ knew this was not true. The one he looked for was orphaned, without a father. Then Buhayra ؈ saw the mark on the boy's back between his shoulder blades and he recognized the mark of prophecy. This boy was the one the world waited for, the one called Ahmad in the Holy Books. Buhayra's ؈ heart filled with joy. He cautioned Abu Talib to take great care of his nephew, to watch over him and protect him. The caravan continued on its way. They traded their goods in Syria and returned safely to Mecca.

Marriage of the Prophet ﷺ

Muhammad ﷺ grew to manhood in his uncle's house. Like the other boys he learned to shoot arrows and fight with a sword. He learned to ride a horse and run fast. He practiced his skills with his uncle Hamza ؓ who was almost his own age. He learned to weigh and measure in order to buy and sell fairly. He learned to deal with people and make peace between them. He protected the weak and defended those unfairly treated. But he never learned to read or to write.

He grew strong and handsome. He had dark almond shaped eyes lined with thick black lashes. He had straight white teeth and a warm smile. His hands were large and strong. His hair was dark and at times came down to his shoulders. He walked with energy and purpose as if walking downhill. He rarely laughed out loud, although he smiled often.

As he grew older he became more serious and thoughtful. He never joined the other boys in rough or useless play. He never made fun of people or told unkind stories and he never, ever lied. He avoided the places where most young men went to play. He spent his time helping his family and those in need. He was known in Mecca as *Al-Amin,* the one you can trust.

His uncle, Abu Talib, and his aunt, 'Atika ؓ, saw that Muhammad ﷺ had grown into a fine young man. Now it was time to look for a suitable wife for him. There was one problem. Abu Talib's business had not been doing well. It took a good amount of money to get married and start a family. Abu Talib

would have given the money to Muhammad ﷺ but Allah had made it so that he had none to give. Abu Talib had hardly enough money to feed his family. So it became clear to them that Muhammad ﷺ needed to look for a job.

'Atika ؓ had a friend whose husband had died and left her a large fortune. This noble lady was beautiful and very intelligent. She had become a businesswoman in her own right. She organized caravans to travel to Syria and Yemen to buy and sell her goods. She hired men to trade for her because she was a noble and modest lady and did not go out into the marketplace. She told them what to buy and where to sell it and for how much. This lady was named Khadija bint Khuwaylid ؓ.

'Atika ؓ went to see Khadija ؓ but was shy to mention the purpose of her visit. She would have left without saying anything if Khadija ؓ had not insisted. Of course Khadija ؓ was very happy to hire 'Atika's ؓ nephew to do her trading. She already had heard a great deal about him. She knew he was known as *Al-Amin*. She knew from her beloved uncle, Waraqa ؓ, a wise man who had read all the Christian and Jewish books, that a prophet was coming. She knew that this prophet was to come from the children of Ismail ﷺ and that there were certain signs that identified him. Her uncle had already picked out Muhammad ﷺ as possibly being that man. So she was very excited to meet him and help him in any way she could.

Khadija ؓ met with Muhammad ﷺ the next day. She talked to him behind a thin curtain but she could see that Muhammad ﷺ had a serious and upright manner. He spoke softly and sensibly. He was modest and polite. She was very impressed. She agreed to send him to Syria with her servant, Maysara ؓ, to be in charge of her business.

The caravan traveled safely. They sold all of Khadija's ؓ goods for high prices and bought the things she wanted for low prices. Maysara ؓ was amazed. In all the years he had done business for Khadija ؓ he had never been

so successful. He began to look at Muhammad ﷺ with great respect. The more he got to know him the more he respected him. He began to notice some unusual things. A cloud always shaded Muhammad ﷺ, traveling above his head. Plants were greener where he passed. Everything he touched seemed to do better than before.

When they returned home Maysara ☾ told Khadija ☽ all he had seen. He told her what a fine and pure and intelligent man this Muhammad ﷺ was. Khadija ☽ was pleased because, after the caravan had left, she had been unable to stop thinking about this young nephew of her friend. She thought to herself that maybe it was possible for there to be a match between them, for she had grown to love him with all her heart and soul. Even though he was only twenty-five and she was almost forty, she looked much younger than her age and he acted much older than his.

Muhammad ﷺ had not really seen Khadija ☽ but had talked with her and knew all about her. He admired her modesty and her intelligence, her fairness and her good sense. But he never thought that such a fine, wealthy and beautiful woman would be interested in a young man without experience or money like himself. He would never have dared to ask for her hand in marriage.

Khadija ☽ realized this and so she decided to express her feelings first. She asked Muhammad ﷺ if he would consider marriage. At first he thought she was teasing him, but then he realized she was serious and his heart leaped with joy. His aunt and uncle, although surprised, were also extremely happy for him. He had found a wife who was even better than any they could have hoped for. Khadija's ☽ uncle, Waraqa ☾, was also very  pleased and so the wedding took place. Khadija ☽ turned over her whole fortune to Muhammad ﷺ, although she did not have to. Khadija ☽ took Muhammad ﷺ as her beloved husband and was content to rely completely on him, whatever might happen.

They lived together in peace and joy for twenty-four years, five months and eight days. They had seven children. Their three boys, Qasim ⸎, Tahir ⸎ and Tayyib ⸎, all died early in childhood. Their four daughters, Zaynab ⸎, Ruqayya ⸎, Umm Kulthum ⸎ and Fatima ⸎, however, grew up to be modest and beautiful young girls and their home was happy and lively.

Muhammad ⸎ had now become an influential man in Mecca. He had money and power. He was intelligent, responsible and generous. He was on his way to becoming the most important young man of Quraysh.

When Muhammad ⸎ was thirty-five the men of Quraysh realized that the Holy Ka'aba needed to be rebuilt. Because it stands in a valley between two mountains, whenever it rained the water drained directly into it. The stones were becoming loose. The Quraysh decided to rebuild it in such a way that it would no longer get flooded.

All the men of Quraysh worked together to take down the massive, stone walls of the Ka'aba. They had torn them down to the height of a man when they

found a green stone and the earth began to shake. They knew they should go no further. This was the foundation laid by Ibrahim ⸎ and Ismail ⸎. Allah wanted that to remain undisturbed.

The Quraysh built the new Ka'aba on the ancient foundation, reusing the same large stones. When it came time to replace the black stone in its corner the men began to argue. They all wanted the honor of being the one to put it back. This stone had been sent by Allah from Paradise for the original Ka'aba built in the time of Adam ⸎. Originally it was all white, but over the centuries it had turned black from the sins of the people who touched it.

The men of Quraysh decided to ask the one they respected most to settle their argument. They went to Muhammad ﷺ, *Al-Amin*. He took his cloak off his shoulders, spread it on the ground, and put the black stone in the center of it. Then he chose one man from each of the four clans of Quraysh to lift a corner of the cloak until the stone was raised to the necessary height. With his own blessed hands, Muhammad ﷺ placed the black stone back in its place in the corner of the Ka'aba where it remains to this day.

7

The Beginning of Prophethood

When he was forty years old something happened that would change forever Muhammad ﷺ and the lives of all those living in Mecca and around the world. All the seeds that Allah had planted since the beginning of time now burst into flower.

It was the custom of the few God-fearing men among the Quraysh to pray and fast in small caves in the hills above Mecca. Muhammad ﷺ began following this practice. As he grew older he spent more and more time alone in the caves meditating on the wonders of Allah and praying. Sometimes he brought some dates and water and stayed several days before returning to his family.

The signs that had surrounded him since childhood became more obvious. He could clearly hear the stones giving him *salams*. He saw the trees bend over him as he walked, as if they were bowing. The wild animals and birds came close to him just to feel his touch. He was wrapped in his love for Allah. He had many dreams and visions. In particular he would see a large figure with a serious face looking at him intently. He had seen this figure many times since he was a child but now he appeared in a larger and more fearsome form.

He was afraid that maybe he was crazy or sick or that it was a devil trying to mislead him. Khadija ﷺ knew immediately that it could not be a sickness for Muhammad ﷺ was too sensible and clear-headed, and it could not

be a devil because he was too pure and good. So she asked him to let her know if the Being came back. Presently the figure returned. Khadija ﴾ removed her headscarf and Muhammad ﷺ told her that the Being had immediately gone away. In this clever way Khadija ﴾ proved to her husband that the figure he saw was good and not evil. An Angel would not stay to look at a woman uncovered in her private room.

One day at the end of the month of *Ramadan* when Muhammad ﷺ was

fasting in the cave on Mt. Hira, overlooking the Ka'aba, the Being he had seen appeared to him again. This time he was enormous. His feet were spread from one side of the horizon to the other. He had a towering body and gigantic wings that filled the whole sky. Muhammad ﷺ would have fallen off the cliff in his fear and amazement if the great figure had not clasped him in his wings and kept him from falling either backwards or forwards.

The enormous figure then greeted Muhammad ﷺ with the words "*Assalamu alaykum, ya Rasulullah.* Peace to you, O Messenger of Allah. I am Jibra'il ﷺ." For this Being was the powerful Archangel himself, Allah's Angelic messenger who had delivered Allah's instructions to all the earlier prophets.

Then hugging the Prophet ﷺ tightly in his wings he told him, "*Iqra* - Read!" Muhammad ﷺ was now gasping for air and could only answer truthfully that he was unable to read. Still the Angel pressed him hard and demanded two more times, "Read!!!" At last the Holy Prophet ﷺ, with great difficulty, gasped, "What shall I read?"

Jibra'il ﷺ then said:
> *Read in the name of your Lord Who has created,*
> *Created man from a clot.*

Read, for your Lord is Most Generous,
Who has taught by the Pen,
Taught man what he knew not. (96:1-5)

This was the first revelation of Allah's book which we call the Quran, and which over the next twenty-three years He would reveal little by little to His Prophet ﷺ and the community of believers.

The Prophet ﷺ repeated these words and only then did Jibra'il ﷺ release him from his embrace. The Prophet ﷺ fell to the ground out of breath and awestruck. He was overwhelmed because no matter who you are, or how great you may be, the Majesty of Allah is so much greater. The Angel disappeared and Muhammad ﷺ hurriedly climbed down the mountain and went home. There he found Khadija ﷺ waiting for him. He looked very pale and tired, and she asked him what had happened. He tried to tell her all he had seen. She knew immediately that what he saw was real, and she became the first to accept the Messenger of Allah.

Muhammad ﷺ was shaking with an intense cold that he felt from the greatness and power of what had just happened to him. He lay down on the couch. Khadija ﷺ covered him with her cloak and he fell asleep.

Khadija ﷺ ran quickly to her uncle, Waraqa ﷺ, to ask his advice. He was excited. He knew that Muhammad ﷺ was the prophet he had been expecting who would bring all the people of the world together in the belief in One God. Waraqa ﷺ felt honored to be the first to recognize him. Khadija ﷺ ran home. She found Muhammad ﷺ still asleep. But in his sleep Jibra'il ﷺ had returned to give him one more piece of Quran. Jibra'il ﷺ said to him:

O you wrapped in your cloak,
Rise up and give warning.
Honor your Lord,
Purify yourself,
Leave unclean things.
Do not give in order to get something in return,

And patiently rely on your Lord. (74: 1-7)

In these first verses Allah taught Muhammad ﷺ the essence of his mission: to warn, to pray, to be generous and kind and, over all, to be patient. Muhammad ﷺ woke up immediately. Khadija ؇ begged him to rest awhile more, but he said his time for rest was over. He must go out and teach whoever would listen, to believe in and pray to Allah.

For the first three years Muhammad ﷺ shared the revelations only with those who showed interest. His nephew 'Ali ؇, Abu Talib's son, who lived in the household of the Prophet ﷺ, was one of the first to believe after Khadija ؇. Slowly other people from his friends and neighbors heard the good news. They would gather together in their houses to hear the verses of Quran that were now being revealed regularly. There were only thirty-nine believers in those early days. They prayed together and worshipped Allah.

The believers were called Muslims, meaning those who are accepting. The poor and weak formed the majority of the early believers. Their hearts were already softened by the difficulties in their lives. They were clearly attracted to the light and warmth that radiated from Muhammad ﷺ.

But not all of the Meccan people were happy about the news of a prophet among them. Many of the rich and powerful were jealous that he had been chosen instead of them. Some refused to accept a leader who they had not chosen themselves. Many others refused to stop worshipping statues that they had carved out of wood or stone with their own hands in order to worship the unseen God who had made them. They clung to the traditions of their fathers and rejected anything new, even if it was better. Allah had sent them so many warnings and so many signs. They were too proud to accept and would bow their heads to the ground for no one.

They began to make the lives of the believers miserable. The owners of believing slaves ordered them to leave Islam and then beat them when they disobeyed. The men of Quraysh would gang up on Muslims they found walking

alone. The women would throw garbage out their windows on the heads of passing Muslims. Even the children would follow them down the street shouting insults.

The beloved Prophet ﷺ himself was hit on the head by a rock and his turban knocked to the ground. He came home one day covered in garbage. His little daughter, Fatima ؓ, burst into tears as she cleaned his face and clothes with her small hands. The people who had respected and trusted him now turned against him and called him a liar.

Oh children, when you hear of these terrible things that happened to your kind and noble Prophet ﷺ, of his pain and sadness, you must let your tears flow. The Angels will join in your weeping. Allah will hear the mournful sound and turn to you with love for He has said that He loves those who love His Beloved.

The First Believers

The group of Muslims was small and weak. The Prophet ﷺ prayed to Allah to send them a man strong and powerful enough to stand up to their enemies. Allah chose 'Umar ibn Khattab ﷺ. Until then 'Umar ﷺ had been one of the biggest enemies of the Muslims. One day he decided to end the trouble once and for all. He strapped on his sword and set out to kill the Prophet ﷺ. On his way he stopped at his sister's house and found that she had become a believer. He was very angry and shouted at her until she let him read some newly revealed verses of Quran. It only called people to goodness and truth. In an instant his heart was changed. 'Umar ﷺ continued on his way to the house where the Prophet ﷺ was teaching. There, to everyone's amazement, he accepted Islam and put his mighty sword at the service of the Muslims.

Now the Muslims had a champion. They felt safe enough to pray openly around the Ka'aba. The Prophet ﷺ took his message to all the people. He recited Quran and taught about Allah publicly. Many young men and women became Muslims as a result. Their parents were upset that their children had abandonned the way that things had been done for generations. Sometimes the parents even locked their believing child inside the house to prevent him from joining the Prophet ﷺ. But despite all their efforts more and more people were hearing the message.

The Prophet ﷺ remained steadfast and patient. The Muslims had no permission to fight back, only to defend themselves. Every day he gently pleaded with his people to listen to the words of Allah. He never showed his anger and never gave up the hope that one day his people would wake up and listen. Always he prayed to Allah for the welfare of all people.

Hamza ؓ, the Prophet's ﷺ uncle and friend, could not stand the unfair treatment of his nephew any longer. He declared his Islam openly. He was a famous lion hunter and he put his great bow at the service of the small Muslim community. He defended the Prophet ﷺ against the anger of his own family and stood up for the Muslims who had little other protection.

Abu Bakr ؓ joined the Muslims. He was a wealthy merchant. He had traveled to Syria with Muhammad ﷺ and knew and loved him. He was a gentle man who was well liked and respected in Mecca. His strength did not lie in the power of his arm but rather in the power of his voice. The Quraysh were eventually forced to come to an agreement with the Muslims in order to stop Abu Bakr ؓ from praying and reciting Quran where he could be heard. His recitation was so full of love and sincerity that those passing by stopped to listen long enough to allow Islam to enter their hearts.

One day the Prophet ﷺ was walking in the desert when he happened upon a Bedouin who was about to kill a gazelle he had captured. This gazelle looked at the Prophet ﷺ with her big brown eyes and spoke to him in human tongue. She told him that she had two babies left in the hills who still did not know how to feed themselves. She asked that the Prophet ﷺ convince the Bedouin to let her go for just five hours. She would run to her children and quickly teach them what plants are good to eat and where to find them. Then she promised to return herself to the hunter.

The Prophet ﷺ spoke to the Bedouin who doubted that any wild animal once set free would return to be eaten. But the Bedouin agreed to set her free on

the condition that the Prophet ﷺ take her place if she failed to return. He would become the property of the Bedouin.

They set the gazelle free and she ran off. After four hours she returned. The Prophet ﷺ asked her why she returned so early. She answered that she was worried the Bedouin might say something unkind to the beloved Prophet ﷺ or that during the wait the Prophet ﷺ might become anxious. Her children had insisted that their mother return. They would survive without her. The Bedouin was speechless. He became Muslim on the spot and then he set the gazelle free.

On another day the Prophet's ﷺ greatest enemy, Abu Jahl, decided that the Meccans needed help in eliminating the new religion that was tearing apart their community. He had the idea to call in the aid of another tribe living nearby. This tribe had a powerful leader named Habib ibn Malik ﷺ. He had a large army that would follow him anywhere. Abu Jahl asked Habib ﷺ to come to Mecca and help him defeat the Prophet ﷺ and the Muslims once and for all.

Habib ﷺ grew very angry when he heard that there was a man claiming to be a prophet who was disrupting a city as important as Mecca. He gathered his warriors behind him and marched on Mecca. On his arrival he demanded that the troublemaker, Muhammad ﷺ, be brought before him.

The Prophet ﷺ wound his black turban around his head and set out on foot alone to meet the angry, warlike Habib ﷺ. Habib ﷺ saw Muhammad ﷺ coming in the distance and he saw the light that radiated around him. His heart opened and filled with belief. Still, to satisfy the others, he asked the Prophet ﷺ to perform two miracles. First he asked that the full moon should rise in the middle of the day. Second he asked that the secret wish hidden in his heart be granted.

The Prophet ﷺ prayed to Allah to help him satisfy Habib ؓ. Allah then made an opening in the sky the size of a pinprick through which the blackness of Hell seeped onto the earth. It was so intensely black that the Quraysh began to shiver and shake and fall over each other in fear. Then the full moon rose until it was high in the sky. At a sign from the holy Prophet ﷺ the moon split into two halves. These two moons spoke loudly so that everyone could hear:

La ilaha ill'Allah Muhammudur Rasulullah.

Then each half slid down to the ground and slipped under the hem of the

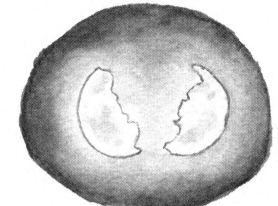

Prophet's ﷺ robe. A different half came out from each of his sleeves and joined together again above his head. Then the moon returned to the place of its rising. The blackness returned to Hell and the sun shone out again over the amazed assembly.

The Prophet ﷺ then told Habib ؓ that he knew his secret wish. Habib ؓ had a daughter who was both crippled and blind. The Prophet ﷺ told him that when he returned home he would find her healed, able to walk and to see.

Habib ؓ took the hand of the Prophet ﷺ and immediately proclaimed his belief. Abu Jahl and the other Quraysh, however, grew even more furious. They said it was a trick and not a true miracle, for no matter what signs Allah sent them they refused to accept. It was as if they were deaf and blind and their hearts were made of stone.

All the warriors in Habib's ؓ army accepted Islam and Habib ؓ returned home. On reaching his house, Habib's ؓ little daughter ran out to greet him, healed and well. Habib ؓ sent two camels loaded with gold and jewels in thanks to the Prophet ﷺ. However, when they arrived in Mecca, Abu Jahl claimed that since he was the chief of Quraysh they belonged to him. Muhammad ﷺ told Abu Jahl to let the camels speak for themselves to whom they had been sent.

Abu Jahl spent the night praying to his idols trying to bribe them with all sorts of presents to do what he wanted. In the morning all the people gathered

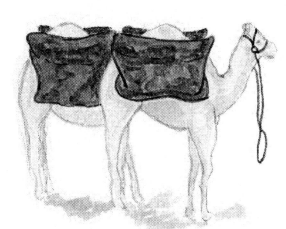

where the camels were stabled. Abu Jahl asked the camels to whom they belonged. The camels continued to chew their food in silence. Then Muhammad ﷺ spoke to them and wiped the end of his woolen cloak over their faces. The camels answered in human language, first with the *shahada,* and then with the clear statement that they belonged to the Prophet of Allah ﷺ.

Still Abu Jahl chose to remain an unbeliever. The Prophet ﷺ accepted the generous gift of Habib ﷺ but he asked Allah to turn the treasure to dust. All the bags of gold and jewels fell to the ground as dry dust. In this way the Prophet ﷺ showed the people that the riches of this world are of no lasting value. What he had to offer them, belief in Allah, was of much more value.

Day by day the situation became more tense in Mecca. The Quraysh decided to try to starve the Muslims into giving up their new religion. No one would buy from them or sell to them. Since this was the only way to get food in Mecca things became very difficult. Their friends and family had to sneak food to the Muslims in the dark of night.

The Prophet ﷺ began looking for a new home for his community where they could live in peace and worship Allah as they wanted. He sent a small group of Muslims across the sea to Abyssinia. The king there was Christian and had invited the believers to live in his country in peace and safety. Some of the Muslims moved to Abyssinia. They hoped that one day all the Muslims together with the Prophet ﷺ would follow. Things were very difficult and the Quraysh did not try to kill the Prophet ﷺ himself only out of respect for his uncle, Abu Talib.

Then the situation became even more difficult. In the tenth year after receiving his prophethood his uncle, Abu Talib, died. Abu Talib had taken care of Muhammad ﷺ since he was a child. Through all the years he had stood

behind him and defended him. Now he was gone. Even worse, he had never declared his Islam because he was afraid of what his old friends might say about him. For this reason the Prophet ﷺ was very sad.

Soon afterwards, in the month of *Ramadan*, Muhammad's ﷺ beloved wife Khadija ؓ also passed away. His daughters lost their mother, and the Prophet ﷺ lost his true companion who always believed in and supported him.

The Prophet ﷺ continued to look for another place to move with his followers. Mecca was becoming too difficult. Their lives were at risk every day. He set out on foot to visit the mountain city of Ta'if. This visit turned into another sadness for the noble Prophet ﷺ. The people there were not interested in what he had to say. They made fun of him and threw stones at him until he had to run for his life.

Returning to Mecca the Prophet ﷺ stopped to rest and pray in the valley of Nakhlah. A company of *Jinn* was passing by. *Jinn* are creatures very much like people except that Allah made them from fire rather than clay. They live in communities as we do but they are invisible to most of us. These *Jinn* heard the Prophet ﷺ reciting the Quran and they stopped to listen. They all became Muslim and returned to their homes to teach their families about Islam.

The Prophet ﷺ was not sent by Allah just for people. In the Quran it says:
We have sent you as a mercy for the worlds. (21:107)
He was sent for the rocks and trees, for the birds and animals, for the fish of the sea. He was sent for all of Allah's creatures, those we know about and those we do not. Allah addresses *Surat ar-Rahman* specifically to both men and *Jinn*.

This journey to Ta'if might appear to have been a great failure, while in fact it was a great success. It brought many, many *Jinn* to Islam. However, the Prophet ﷺ was still worried. He had found no place to resettle the Muslim people still suffering in Mecca. The Prophet ﷺ returned to Mecca more troubled

than when he had left, saddened and a little unsure. His wife and his uncle were no longer there to comfort and support him. The future of his mission looked uncertain. He wondered what Allah had in store for him.

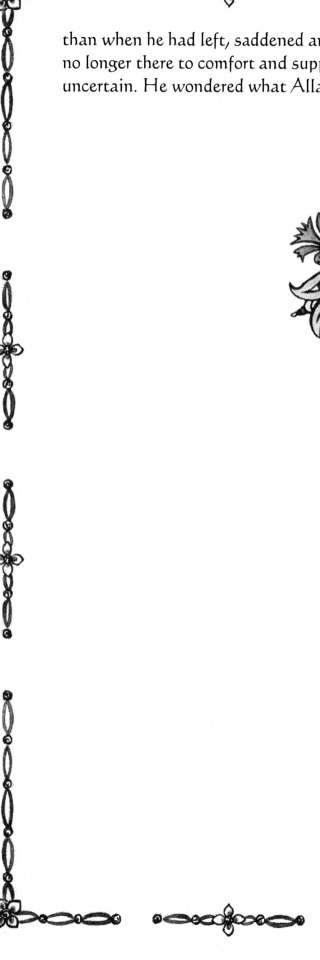

Isra—The Night Journey

At this, the lowest point in his life, the beloved Prophet ﷺ went to the Ka'aba to seek comfort in prayer. He prayed and then sat to meditate. Abu Jahl, the enemy of God, and his gang found the Prophet ﷺ there alone. They began to insult him and taunt him in their overwhelming pride and ignorance. This made the Prophet ﷺ even more sad. He felt that it was his fault that they could not see the truth. He was offering the most precious gift in all the worlds, Islam, and they acted as if he were offering them dirt. Why, he wondered, was he unable to make them understand?

He left the Ka'aba heavy-hearted and went to visit Abu Talib's daughter, Umm Hani ﵂, who still lived nearby in her father's house between the hills of *Safa* and *Marwa*. She was only able to give him a little comfort. She prepared a clean rug for him in the courtyard. He prayed the night prayer and in his deepening sadness lay down to sleep.

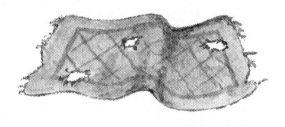

It was a Monday night, the twenty-seventh of the month of *Rajab*. Allah Almighty looked down at His beloved, lying sad and tired on a threadbare rug in the courtyard of Umm Hani's ﵂ house. The Lord of Mercy then called Jibra'il ﵇ and told him to alert the Angels and residents of Paradise that the time had come. Mika'il ﵇ was ordered to stop measuring out provisions for mankind. Israfil ﵇ was commanded to put down his great trumpet. Azra'il ﵇ was prohibited from taking a single soul in death. For three hours all the Heavens

were to be garlanded with jewel-like flowers and crystal lights, and the gates of the Hells were to be tightly shut.

Allah Almighty ordered Jibra'il ﷺ to go to the green pastures of Paradise and choose a *Buraq* steed. From there he must quickly go to the side of the Holy Prophet ﷺ and awaken him gently. Tonight was to be the night of the fulfillment of his destiny. Allah, Merciful and Majestic, was inviting His beloved on a journey passing through the Seven Heavens and the gardens of Paradise to a place to which none other of His creation had ever been before. Allah was bringing the Prophet ﷺ to Himself.

Jibra'il ﷺ went to the pastures of paradise where he saw thousands of *Buraqs* grazing and playing. A *Buraq* looks a little like a pure white horse with a flowing mane. Some say its tail resembles the feathers of a peacock in its design

 and beauty. Its hooves are of coral, its feet of gold. Its chest is of red ruby while its back and sides are of pearl. It has two great wings decorated with rubies. Some say its mane is laced with pearls and its ears with green emeralds. Others say it has a face like a beautiful woman. In any case its eyes are like stars that sparkle like the sun and its beauty cannot be described completely by anyone except Allah Almighty Himself. The *Buraq* speaks in a pure Arabic language.

Jibra'il ﷺ noticed that one *Buraq* was not playing and racing about like the others. His head hung down and tears streamed from his eyes. Jibra'il ﷺ asked this *Buraq* the reason for his sadness. The *Buraq* answered that one day while he was prancing in the paradise pasture with the others he heard a voice that called out: "Ya Muhammad ﷺ!" At the sound of this name all desire for playing and games left his heart. He longed only to see this one called Muhammad ﷺ. It was now forty thousand years since he had heard the mention of that beloved

one, and still this *Buraq* could think of nothing but Muhammad ﷺ. He did not want to gallop into the wind or graze on the grass of Paradise. He wanted only to hear some news of his beloved Muhammad ﷺ.

This was the *Buraq* that Jibra'il ﷺ chose. He saddled him with a saddle of light and placed a bridle of green chrysolite over his head. "Let us go," said Jibra'il ﷺ, "to your beloved Muhammad ﷺ as fast as we can fly." The *Buraq* sprang into the air, his heart racing and his eyes flashing. He did as he was commanded, with joy.

Within the blink of an eye they were standing at the feet of the Prophet ﷺ, sleeping in the humble house of Umm Hani ﷺ. Jibra'il ﷺ called to him gently to awake and come with them. They were bringing him greetings of peace and an invitation from the Lord of the Worlds.

The Prophet ﷺ arose and made his *wudu'* in water that had been brought from the stream of *Kawthar* that flows in Paradise. Jibra'il ﷺ poured the water from ruby pitchers into a bowl of green emerald that was shaped with four corners. In each corner was a jewel that shone like the sun and lit up the night sky. After he had washed, the Angel dressed him in a robe of pure light and set a turban of forty thousand folds of light upon his head. Then Jibra'il ﷺ fastened a cape of light around his shoulders and a belt of rubies around his waist. He placed in his hand a whip of green emeralds decorated with four hundred pearls, each of which shone like the morning star.

Then they proceeded to the Ka'aba and prayed at the station of Ibrahim ﷺ. All the Angels, beginning with the Archangels, came to see him and give him their greetings of peace. After that Jibra'il ﷺ asked the Prophet ﷺ to mount the *Buraq* ﷺ and begin the journey.

Jibra'il ﷺ held the reins while the Prophet ﷺ put his blessed foot in the ruby stirrup. The *Buraq* ﷺ thought he would burst from joy. The desire of his heart had been fulfilled and yet he found that seeing his beloved Muhammad ﷺ

and smelling his sweet scent had only increased the burning love in his heart. He shifted his feet in discomfort. Jibra'il ﷺ scolded him for moving even a little as the Prophet ﷺ was mounting him. The poor *Buraq* ﷺ blushed with shame and begged forgiveness. He needed to ask something of Muhammad ﷺ. The Prophet ﷺ smiled kindly and told him to ask. The *Buraq* ﷺ could not bear that this would be the only time he would carry the Holy Prophet ﷺ. He asked if he could be the *Buraq* ﷺ to carry Muhammad ﷺ on the Last Day from his resting place to the place of Gathering. The Prophet ﷺ smiled and promised the *Buraq* ﷺ that he would be chosen on that day also. Then the Prophet ﷺ mounted and the *Buraq* ﷺ stepped forward with majesty and strength, for he was carrying the light of the worlds upon his back. His heart filled with joy because he knew that another day would come when he would carry his beloved once again.

His ruby studded wings unfolded and with each step the *Buraq* ﷺ traveled as far as the eye could see. Jibra'il ﷺ flew at his right stirrup with seventy thousand angels behind him. Mika'il ﷺ flew at his left stirrup with

another seventy thousand angels. Behind them came Israfil ﷺ and seventy thousand more angels behind him. Every angel held a candlestick of glowing light. For the whole journey the feet of the *Buraq* ﷺ never touched the ground. When his golden feet did touch down they stepped lightly on fine flowered silks from Paradise with which the angels had carpeted the earth.

They paused on their journey four times to pray. The first time was at the village of Yathrib that was to become the Prophet's ﷺ city, Medina. The second time was at the well where Musa ﷺ drew water for Shu'ayb's ﷺ daughters. The third time was on top of Mount Sinai where Allah spoke to Musa ﷺ. The fourth time was at the spot where Maryam ﷺ gave birth to the Prophet 'Isa ﷺ.

On this journey the Prophet ﷺ saw and heard many extraordinary things, some of which he told us and some of which he did not. Then they arrived at Jerusalem. All the angels followed the *Buraq* ﷺ as it set down in front of the *Masjid ul-Aqsa,* the Farthest Mosque, where the temple of Sulaiman ﷺ used to stand. The angels assembled there called out: "Greetings to you who are the first. Greetings to you who are the last. Greetings to you who will gather all men together." Muhammad ﷺ was called the first because Allah created his light before anything else. He was called the last because he was the last prophet to be sent. He was called the gatherer of men because he was the only one to call all the people of the whole world to assemble under one banner, Islam, and those who do, on the Day of Judgment, will be safe.

The Holy Prophet ﷺ dismounted at the gates of the *Masjid ul-Aqsa.* Jibra'il ﷺ tethered the *Buraq* ﷺ to a ring to which all the earlier prophets had tied their mounts. The souls of all the prophets then came to give greetings of peace to their brother Muhammad ﷺ. One by one they took his hand and asked Allah's blessings for him. Jibra'il ﷺ gave the *iqama* and the Prophet ﷺ was ordered to lead them all in prayer. The angels and the prophets arranged themselves in straight rows and followed Muhammad ﷺ in prayer. After this he turned to face them and raised his hands to ask Allah to forgive the weakness and forgetfulness of those who would follow him. All the prophets joined him in saying, "*Amin.*" Allah spoke and granted his prayer.

The Angel Jibra'il ﷺ then appeared beside him holding a tray on which were three cups. One cup was full of wine, one full of water, and one full of white, frothy milk. The Prophet ﷺ picked up the cup of  milk and drank it down until only a few drops remained. Then he handed it back. Jibra'il ﷺ told Muhammad ﷺ that he had chosen the drink most suitable for his nation of Islam. If, however, he had finished all the milk down to the last drop not a single member of the Muslim nation would have to experience the punishments of Hell. The Prophet ﷺ asked Jibra'il ﷺ to return the cup so that he could finish the last drops. But Jibra'il ﷺ, by the command of his Lord, answered that what was written since the beginning of time had come to pass.

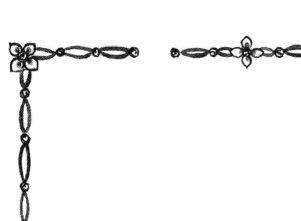

Mi'raj—The First Heaven

Jibra'il ﷺ led the Prophet ﷺ out of the *Masjid ul-Aqsa* to a rock on a hill. There they saw the foot of a ladder that reached up to the sky and disappeared in the clouds. One side rail was made of ruby and the other of emerald. The treads were of gold and silver, each one decorated with different precious stones in an intricate design. This ladder is called the Stairway of the Angels because it is the way angels come and go between Heaven and Earth. Azra'il ﷺ, the Angel of Death, descends these steps to take the souls of mankind. The dying see the glimmering treads of this beautiful ladder and in their  wide-eyed amazement they forget the sorrows of death. Azra'il ﷺ leads their souls up the steps to the First Heaven.

The Prophet ﷺ was invited to climb this ladder while he was still living. Jibra'il ﷺ took Muhammad ﷺ within the protection of his wings and prepared to follow him up the stairs. As the Prophet ﷺ stood on the ground his foot rested on a large stone that proceeded to raise itself up, gently lifting him to the first step. It would have continued to rise, never wanting to lose the touch of his foot,

except that the Prophet ﷺ ordered it to stay. The rock obeyed, immediately stopping where it was, hanging in midair. To this day it remains suspended over the place where the ladder had stood, and a beautiful mosque has been built around it. If a simple stone can defy gravity in order to obey the Prophet's ﷺ command, how can we be less obedient?

And so the Prophet ﷺ rose into the sky, each gracious step of the ladder lifting him gently to the next step. They traveled up and up until they came to an immense, stormy ocean the water of which is suspended between sky and earth. When you look at the sun and see the shimmering of its light, it is really the waves of this ocean that you are seeing.

They continued to travel upwards until they reached the home of the Wind. The Wind is bound tightly with seventy thousand strong chains. Seventy thousand angels hold firmly to each chain to keep the Wind under control. The Prophet ﷺ and Jibra'il ﷺ continued to move up until they passed out of the earthly atmosphere. This looked like it was made of green emerald but is in fact made of steam and water.

After a distance that would take a man five hundred years to travel they reached the gate of the First Heaven, called the Gate of Protection. It is made

of red ruby and its lock is of pearl. Jibra'il ﷺ knocked at the gate and a tremendous voice asked, "Who knocks at my gate?" Jibra'il ﷺ answered: "It is I, Jibra'il ﷺ, and with me is the Prophet Muhammad ﷺ." "Welcome, welcome to you," cried the voice, and the gates swung open.

Standing before them was Isma'il ﷺ appearing as a mighty warrior riding on a huge horse of light. One hundred thousand angel warriors surrounded him on all sides and each one of these had another hundred thousand soldiers at his command. Together with Isma'il ﷺ they glorified the Almighty Lord in a thunderous chorus.

The Prophet ﷺ greeted Isma'il ﷺ and his army of angels. He asked about the form of prayer in which he saw them standing, *qiyam*. Because he liked it so

much, *qiyam* was given to him to be part of the prayer of the Muslims. Beyond the army of Isma'il ﷺ were some angels made of wind and water. Their commander was called Ra'd ﷺ, which means thunder. He controls rain and storms and from his mouth issues thunder and lightening. This First Heaven was so full of praying angels that the Prophet ﷺ could hardly find the space in which to walk.

Then they saw an amazing sight. There was an Angel named Habib ﷺ who was shaped like a man, but from the waist up he was made of snow and from the waist down he was made of fire. The fire did not melt the snow and the snow did not put out the fire. Tears were streaming down his face. His hands were raised on high and he implored his Lord, saying, "O Allah, Who has united fire and snow, unite the hearts of the believers."

They greeted Habib ﷺ and passed on until they came to a figure draped in robes of light seated on a throne of light. On either side of the throne was a closed door. This was the Prophet Adam ﷺ, the father of mankind. Whenever a person dies his soul is presented before Adam ﷺ. If it was a good and believing soul Adam ﷺ is pleased and says, "A pure soul from a pure body," and that soul is taken through the door on his right to *Illiyun* in the Highest Heaven. Whenever an unbelieving soul is presented, Adam ﷺ becomes angry and shouts, "An impure soul from an impure body," and the angels drag that soul through the door on his left to a terrible place called *Sijjin*.

Adam ﷺ rose to his feet in great joy when he saw the Prophet Muhammad ﷺ approaching and he greeted him with love. Adam ﷺ thanked Allah for giving him such a righteous son. Muhammad ﷺ thanked Allah for giving him such a father, the *qibla* to whom all the angels had been ordered to bow. In reply, Adam ﷺ said humbly that this honor had been given to him only on account of the light of Muhammad ﷺ that had been placed upon his brow.

After spending some time together with Adam ﷺ, Jibra'il ﷺ and Muhammad ﷺ gave their *salams* and continued on. The next angel they saw had the shape of a rooster but he was so enormous that his head reached the Divine Throne and his feet were planted below the Earth. The rooster's two

wings, when spread, reached from the farthest East to the farthest West. This rooster is pure, unspeckled white, like pearl, and the comb on his head is ruby red. Jibra'il ﷺ told him that this is the Rooster of the Divine Throne. It is he who calls the heavenly *adhan* to alert all the angels that it is time to pray. In the last third of the night he descends close to the earth, flaps his great wings and calls out, "O you who would worship, arise and pray!" The roosters on Earth, in the barns and farmyards, hear this Angel's call. They too begin to flap their wings and call. At the time of the *fajr* prayer the Rooster of the Divine Throne calls again and all the roosters on Earth echo his call. "Arise, O you forgetful ones," they say. "Arise and pray for forgiveness."

On the Last Day of all days the Rooster of the Divine Throne will begin his call as usual, but Allah will tell him to be silent. The night will continue for the length of three days and three nights and neither roosters will crow nor dogs will bark. Those who were used to rising and praying will awaken and pray for

forgiveness. The | forgetful ones will sleep on as
if nothing were | happening. When the day
finally dawns the | sun will rise in the western sky
and the chance to | ask for forgiveness will be gone
forever.

It is said to | be a very good thing to keep an
actual white rooster | near your house. Not only will
it wake you for | prayer but it will protect you
and your neighbors | from harm. The Prophet ﷺ
said, "The white | rooster is my dear and beloved

friend and he is the enemy of my enemy."

Then they journeyed on until they came to a sea whose waters are milky white and thick like cream. This Jibra'il ﷺ said is called the Sea of Life. On the day when all creatures will be called to rise from their graves, Allah will cause a rain to fall consisting of the water of this sea. Whatever is buried in the Earth will instantly return to its original state as soon as this water touches it. What had long been scattered will come together. All the bones and dust of people long gone will rise again, just as they once were, and stand before their Lord for judgment.

Before they moved on, Jibra'il ﷺ called the *adhan* and the Prophet ﷺ led all the inhabitants of the First Heaven in prayer.

11

The Second And Third Heavens

The journey between each heaven is the distance of five hundred years traveling, and yet, in the twinkling of an eye, Jibra'il 🕊 and the Prophet ﷺ stood before the gate of the Second Heaven. The gate was made of pearls and its lock of light. This Heaven was so bright that it caused the Holy Prophet ﷺ to squint his eyes to avoid being blinded by it. The name of this Heaven is *Qaydum* and it is made mostly of red coral.

Jibra'il 🕊 knocked at the gate. The Archangel Mika'il 🕊 answered and asked who desired to enter. Jibra'il 🕊 replied, "It is I, Jibra'il 🕊, and with me is the Prophet Muhammad ﷺ." "Welcome, welcome to you, O honored guests," said Mika'il 🕊 and he opened wide the gates.

Inside they saw Mika'il 🕊 with two hundred thousand angels all at his service and each one of those had another two hundred thousand to help him. They greeted each other and praised the Glorious Lord Who created so many wondrous things. Behind them Muhammad ﷺ saw rows and rows of angels all in the position of bowing, *ruku'*. They did not move. They had remained bent in this position since the day they were created, reciting the praises of their Creator, the Lord of Glory and Might. The Prophet ﷺ was so impressed by this that *ruku'* was also given to him to be part of the prayer of the Muslims.

Then they saw two young men who introduced themselves as the Prophets Yahya 🕊, son of Zakariyya 🕊, and 'Isa 🕊, son of Maryam ﷻ. 'Isa 🕊

was fair and smiling but Yahya ﷺ was more stern and serious. They greeted the Prophet ﷺ warmly as their loving brother and told him of the many blessings his Lord had waiting for him ahead.

Muhammad ﷺ and Jibra'il ﷺ continued on until their way was blocked by a very great Angel. He had seventy thousand heads. On each head there were seventy thousand faces. Each face had seventy thousand mouths and in every mouth there were seventy thousand tongues. Each of these tongues spoke an entirely different language and with each of these tongues the angel glorified Allah. The Prophet ﷺ was amazed and asked Jibra'il ﷺ about this Angel. Jibra'il ﷺ told him that the Angel is named Qasim ﷺ and that it is his job to distribute to each created being its daily provision, its measured portion of food and wealth, no more, no less.

Passing beyond Qasim ﷺ, Muhammad ﷺ beheld an even more wondrous Angel. He was seated on a throne of light which had four corners, each of which was supported by seven hundred thousand pillars of gold and silver. Around him were angels beyond count. To his right were seventy thousand angels ranged in rows, dressed in green and glowing with light. They were so beautiful it was almost impossible to look at them. Even their scent and their words were beautiful and sweet. To his left were another seventy thousand angels ranged in rows. Their faces were angry and fearsome. Their look was dark and vengeful. Their clothing was ugly and their smell disgusting. Even their speech was rough and rude. When they praised Allah their mouths erupted in flames. Their eyes were so cold and cruel that it was almost impossible to look at them. The great

Angel on the throne was covered head to foot with eyes. Before him was a Tablet of stone, the *Lawh ul-Mahfudh*. In front of that grew an enormous tree so thick with leaves that only Allah could count them. On each leaf was written the name of a person.

The Prophet ﷺ, trembling with awe, asked Jibra'il ﷺ to tell him the name of this great Angel. Jibra'il ﷺ replied that it was Azra'il ﷺ, the Angel of Death. The tree was the Tree of Life. When a baby is born a new leaf, on which the name of the newborn

is written, buds out from a branch of this tree. During his lifetime the leaf unfurls and becomes glossy and green. When his life is ending, his leaf begins to yellow and wither. When the leaf falls Azra'il ﷺ gives it to angels who mix it into the person's food. In this way he is given forewarning that it is time to set his affairs in order and prepare for death. On the day, at the hour and minute that is written, his name is erased from the Tablet. Azra'il ﷺ stretches out his hand and takes the person's soul wherever he is, east or west. If his soul is among the blessed, Azra'il ﷺ hands it to the angels on the right who are the Angels of Mercy. If the soul has darkened itself with unbelief and unkind actions it is handed to the angels on the left who teach it a hard lesson about what it did wrong.

Muhammad ﷺ became afraid for he knew the weakness and forgetfulness of those who would follow him. He begged Azra'il ﷺ to please take the souls of his nation gently. Azra'il ﷺ answered that Allah, Lord of Majesty and Might, calls to him seventy times during every day reminding him to treat the souls of the nation of His beloved Muhammad ﷺ with kindness and forgiveness. The Prophet ﷺ breathed a sigh of relief and thanked Allah. Jibra'il ﷺ called the *adhan* and Muhammad ﷺ led all those assembled in the Second Heaven in prayer.

Then they proceeded to the Third Heaven. It was a distance of five hundred years journeying, but they arrived in the blink of an eye. The gate is made of pearl with a lock of light. Jibra'il ﷺ knocked and a voice demanded to know who desired to enter. Jibra'il ﷺ answered, "It is I, Jibra'il ﷺ, and with me is the Prophet Muhammad ﷺ." Arina'il ﷺ, the keeper of the gates, opened them wide and said, "Welcome, welcome to you, O worthy guests." This heaven is made up mostly of copper and its name is *Zaytun*.

Beyond Arina'il ﷺ were row upon row of angels bowed low to the ground in *sajda*. In this position they remained for all time, praising Allah, the Most High. They only raised their heads up briefly to answer the greetings of the Prophet ﷺ. Muhammad ﷺ was so pleased by this form of prayer that *sajda* was also given to him to be part of the prayer of the Muslims. Because the angels looked up once and then bowed their heads again, *sajda* is performed twice in each *rak'a* of prayer.

They passed on and came into the presence of a very handsome and shining figure. This was the Prophet Yusuf ﷺ. Of all the beauty existing in the whole world, Yusuf ﷺ was given half. He took time from his praising of the Lord of Beauty and Majesty to welcome the Prophet ﷺ with much dignity and warmth. He prayed for him and for the Muslims.

Then they encountered the Prophets Da'ud ﷺ and Sulaiman ﷺ, father and son, who together prayed to Allah, Lord of Light, King of Kings. They advised Muhammad ﷺ and prayed for him.

Then the Prophet ﷺ saw a really fearsome Angel. He was called Malik ﷺ and he and eighteen others are keepers of the Seven Hells. Just as Allah has created seven Heavens for the blessed to enjoy, and seven Earths for the living to be tested, so He has created seven Hells for the doers of evil to be punished. The Prophet ﷺ was given a small glimpse of the First Hell. He began to tremble and tears of pity and sorrow rolled down his blessed cheeks because of the terrible things he saw. The Archangels Jibra'il ﷺ and Mika'il ﷺ and the *Muqarrabin* ﷺ, who are the Angels of Closeness, began to weep also because of his distress.

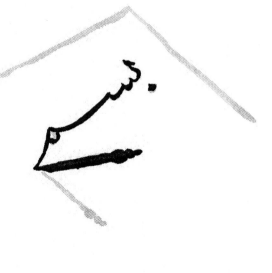

Allah Almighty, Lord of Forgiveness and Mercy, in order to ease his sorrow, promised the Prophet ﷺ that he will be able to lead whoever he wishes out of Hell. Allah also gave him the news that in the Quran there are nineteen letters that will protect those who recite them from the nineteen keepers of Hell. These letters form the phrase: *Bismillahir Rahmanir Rahim.*

Then Malik ﷺ closed the door to Hell so tightly that none of its heat or smoke or darkness could leak through. Jibra'il ﷺ called the *adhan* and all the angels and inhabitants of the Third Heaven prayed behind Muhammad *Rasulullah* ﷺ.

59

The Fourth, Fifth, Sixth, And Seventh Heavens

Five hundred years of traveling was accomplished in the twinkling of an eye. Jibra'il ﷺ and the Prophet Muhammad ﷺ stood before the gate of the Fourth Heaven. Its gate is made of light its lock is also of light. This heaven is made of pure silver and it is called *Zahir*. Jibra'il ﷺ knocked and a voice from within asked who was there. Jibra'il ﷺ answered as before, "It is I, Jibra'il ﷺ, and with me is the Prophet Muhammad ﷺ." The large gate swung open and they came face to face with a massive angel named Salsa'il ﷺ. "Welcome, welcome to you, O awaited guests," he said.

Salsa'il ﷺ is the commander of four hundred thousand angel troops. They are arranged in ranks, some standing in *qiyam*, some bending in *ruku'*, and others with their foreheads to the ground in *sajda*. The Prophet ﷺ saw that the ones standing and bowing never looked left or right. In *qiyam* they only looked steadily at the spot their heads would touch in *sajda*, and in *ruku'* they kept their eyes focused on a point between their feet. The ones in *sajda* were so concentrated on their prayer that their eyes never left looking at their noses. The Prophet ﷺ was very impressed with the rapt devotion and unswerving attention of those angels, so much so that this manner of directing the eyes was given to him and his nation for their prayer.

Then they met the Prophets Idris and Nuh. They greeted each other like long lost brothers. They met Maryam, the mother of 'Isa, and Buhayyid, the mother of Musa, and Asiya, the wife of Pharaoh. Maryam had seventy thousand mansions all made of pearl. Buhayyid had seventy

thousand mansions all made of green emeralds. Asiya had seventy thousand mansions made of red coral.

Jibra'il called the *adhan* and the Prophet led all the angels and inhabitants of the Fourth Heaven in prayer.

They journeyed on for the distance of five hundred years until they came before the gates of the Fifth Heaven, which is called *Safiya* and is made of red gold. Jibra'il knocked and a voice asked who desired entrance. Jibra'il replied, "It is I, Jibra'il, and with me is the Prophet Muhammad." The gates swung open and they found Kalqa'il, the guardian of this Heaven seated on a throne of light. They greeted each other with peace. Around this throne were angel helpers too numerous to count.

Some of the angels were seated on their knees in *qa'da*. They had been praying in this way since the day they were created. Their eyes were fixed on their knees and they were giving their full attention to the praise they recited of their Creator. The Prophet was so pleased with this form of worship that *qa'da* was given to him and his nation for their prayer.

They continued on until they reached the shore of a limitless ocean. Jibra'il said that this dark sea is called the Sea of Vengeance. It is from these waters that the flood of Nuh was ordered to descend. Here Jibra'il called the *adhan* and all the inhabitants of the Fifth Heaven followed the Prophet Muhammad in prayer.

Faster than light they journeyed the distance of five hundred years traveling until they reached the Sixth Heaven. This Heaven is made from

yellow topaz and its name is *Khalisa*. Jibra'il ﷺ knocked at the gates and was asked to identify himself. He said, "It is I, Jibra'il ﷺ, and with me is the Prophet Muhammad ﷺ." "Welcome, welcome to you awaited guests," said a voice and the gates opened wide. Inside they met Samkha'il ﷺ, the Angel guardian of the Sixth Heaven. Samkha'il ﷺ blessed the Prophet ﷺ and wished him well in his mission.

Jibra'il ﷺ and Muhammad ﷺ continued their journey. They met the *Muqarrabin*, the Angels of Closeness, called cherubim in English. There were countless numbers of them, all reciting their *dhikr* and praising Allah. Passing beyond them they met Musa ﷺ. The Prophet ﷺ greeted him and Musa ﷺ rose from his place and kissed the Prophet ﷺ between the eyes. He rejoiced that this night Muhammad ﷺ was invited to an intimate meeting with his Lord. But Musa ﷺ warned him not to forget the weakness of his nation. If any obligations were to be placed on his followers, Muhammad ﷺ should try to make them as few as possible. As the Prophet ﷺ was leaving, Musa ﷺ began to weep.

Passing on they met the Archangel Mika'il ﷺ. Seated on an enormous throne he was weighing things on a huge scale, the balance of which was so large it could have held all the Heavens and Earths. He said, "Happy are the ones who follow you, O Muhammad ﷺ, because their weight on the scales is

greater than any other nation." Around Mika'il ﷺ were so many angels that the eye became exhausted looking for the end of them. One of these angels is assigned to watch over each drop of rain and snow, each fruit and growing plant. When he has done his job he never works again. Every living thing has a new and different angel assigned to it until the end of time.

The *dhikr* of Mika'il ﷺ is: "*Subhana Rabbil A'la*, Glory to the Lord Most High." If a believer recites this during his life, when his time comes to die Mika'il ﷺ will send an Angel of Mercy to him and he will be safe from all fear. That is why the Holy Prophet ﷺ taught us to say this three times when we make *sajda* during prayer.

Then they reached a luminous green sea covered with angels glorifying the Most Generous Lord. Jibra'il ﷺ called the *adhan* and the Prophet ﷺ led all the inhabitants of the Sixth Heaven in prayer.

Now Jibra'il ﷺ and the Prophet Muhammad ﷺ covered the distance of five hundred years traveling in one instant and arrived in front of the gates of the Seventh Heaven. This Heaven is made entirely from light and its name is *Ghariba*. Jibra'il ﷺ knocked and Afra'il ﷺ, the gatekeeper, answered. Jibra'il ﷺ announced, "It is I, Jibra'il ﷺ, and with me is the Prophet Muhammad ﷺ." Afra'il ﷺ opened the gates with joy and they saw him surrounded by seven hundred thousand angels, all under his command.

Then they saw an Angel with seven hundred thousand heads. Each head had seven hundred thousand faces. Each face had seven hundred thousand mouths. In each mouth there were seven hundred thousand tongues, each speaking seven hundred thousand languages. This Angel also had seven hundred thousand wings. Every day he plunges seven hundred thousand times into an ocean of light that is in Paradise. Each time he comes out of the ocean he shakes himself. From every drop of light that flies off of his feathers the Almighty Lord creates another angel who glorifies his Creator.

They continued on until they came to a great Angel whose feet stood on the lowest Earth and whose head touched the Divine Throne. He was so gigantic that he could have swallowed the world and all that is in it in one gulp. The tip of one wing touched the farthest East and the tip of the other touched the farthest West. Seven hundred thousand angels were at his service. This was the Archangel Israfil ﷺ. They greeted each other with dignity and warmth.

Still they journeyed on until they came to a person seated on a throne of nobility bathed in light. At his feet sat many smiling and contented children. This was the Prophet Ibrahim ﷺ and, because of his great love for the nation of Muhammad ﷺ, all the souls of the Muslim children who die before they are

grown are entrusted to him. Ibrahim ﷺ teaches them and takes care of them until the Day of Gathering. Then he will lead them into the Presence of their Lord Who will invite them to enter Paradise. These children, however, will only consent to go when their parents have been forgiven and can go with them. Allah will forgive the parents because of the children and they will enter Paradise together.

Ibrahim ﷺ and Muhammad ﷺ exchanged heartfelt greetings. Ibrahim ﷺ then gave him a message for the Muslims. He said to tell them that the world

is worth less than the wing of a fly but that their Lord's Pleasure is of immense value. They should spend their time on Earth planting trees in Paradise that they will be able to enjoy for eternity. The Prophet ﷺ asked how they could plant these trees in Paradise while they still lived on Earth. Ibrahim ﷺ replied that each time believers recite the following prayer a tree is planted for them in Paradise. The prayer is:

Subhan Allahi wal hamdulillahi
Wa la ilaha ill'Allahu wa Allahu akbar
Wa la hawla wala quwwata illa billahil 'aliyyal 'adhim.

"Glory to Allah to Whom all Praise is due. There is no god but Allah. Allah is most Great. There is no might and no power except that of Allah, the Exalted, the Majestic."

Then they traveled on until they came to the *Bayt ul-Ma'mur*. This Holy House is the same size and shape as the Ka'aba in Mecca. Were it to be lowered down to the Earth it would land exactly on the roof of the Ka'aba. Allah made it from rubies and it has two doors each made of emerald. It is lit by ten thousand lamps of gold. It has a minaret of pure silver which is as high as the distance between the heavens. In front of it is a sea of light in which the angel pilgrims of the Seventh Heaven bathe before they wrap themselves in an *ihram* of light. Then they go round about the *Bayt ul-Ma'mur* calling, "*Labbayk*

Allahuma labbayk, at Your service, O Lord, at Your service," just like the pilgrims on Earth make *tawaf* around the Ka'aba.

All the angels gather here to pray on Fridays. Jibra'il ﷺ calls the *adhan.* Israfil ﷺ gives the *khutba.* Mika'il ﷺ leads the prayer. The Prophet ﷺ liked this gathering for prayer so much that the Friday congregational prayer was given to him to be part of the worship of his nation. Whoever joins in *Juma'a* prayer receives the blessings of all the praying angels and the promise of forgiveness by Allah Almighty. On this night the angels asked the Prophet Muhammad ﷺ to lead them in prayer. So Jibra'il ﷺ made the *adhan* and Muhammad ﷺ led all the angels in prayer in front of the *Bayt ul-Ma'mur* in the Seventh Heaven.

Sidrat ul-Muntaha

Then Jibra'il ﷺ and the Prophet Muhammad ﷺ journeyed on until they arrived at a place beyond which none had gone before. It is called *Sidrat ul-Muntaha*, which means the Lotus Tree of the Farthest Boundary. It is a tree of gold with branches of emerald and ruby. The tree is so tall it would take a man one hundred and fifty years to climb to the top. Its leaves are large and rounded like the ears of an elephant. A single one of them could blanket the entire world as we know it. It has fruits that are shaped like water jars and the whole tree is bathed in a radiant light. On each leaf there are as many angels as there are stars in the sky and they glow and flutter like golden butterflies all over the tree. When they saw the Prophet ﷺ they sang, full of wonder at his beauty, thanking Allah for giving them sight of him.

The home of Jibra'il ﷺ is on one of the emerald branches of this tree. On the branch is a carpet woven of light and on that is a *mihrab* of red ruby. This is the prayer place of Jibra'il ﷺ. In front of the *mihrab* is a seat of honor, which belongs to the Prophet Muhammad ﷺ and upon which no other had ever been permitted to sit until then. Jibra'il ﷺ invited the Prophet ﷺ to sit. All around them were countless angels reciting Allah's Books, the Torah of Musa ﷺ, the *Zabur* of Da'ud ﷺ, the *Injil* of 'Isa ﷺ and the Holy Quran.

It was here that Muhammad ﷺ saw for the first time the true form of his familiar companion, Jibra'il ﷺ. He had six hundred wings decorated in pearls and multicolored jewels. It would have taken a bird seven hundred years to fly from one of his shoulders to the other. When he spread his wings he filled all the space from East to West. Jibra'il ﷺ asked the Prophet ﷺ to do him honor by leading a prayer in his home. Muhammad ﷺ led all the angels of the *Sidrat ul-Muntaha* in prayer.

At the foot of this tree flow four streams. Two of them are clearly visible and two of them, arising from one source, *Salsabil*, are hidden. The two visible streams flow down to the Earth and become the Euphrates and the Nile. The two hidden streams flow into Paradise and are named *Kawthar* (Abundance) and *Rahma* (Mercy). The river *Kawthar* belongs to the Prophet Muhammad ﷺ. Its water is whiter than milk, sweeter than honey, more perfumed than musk. On entering Paradise the blessed souls drink from the river *Kawthar* and all their bad habits and heartaches disappear. Then they bathe in the river *Rahma* and become young and beautiful. The men become thirty-three years old, tall and strong with green beards. The women become young, beautiful maidens and they never grow old again.

Near the tree was another great Angel. He had seventy thousand heads. Each head had seventy thousand faces. Every face had seventy thousand mouths. Each head was covered with seventy thousand coverings, which were decorated with a thousand times a thousand pearls. Each of these pearls was so big that it appeared as a globe containing a whole ocean with all its swimming creatures inside. This Angel recited, *"La ilaha ill'Allah, Muhammadur Rasulullah,"* with such a beautiful voice that even the Divine Throne trembled at the sound of it.

The Prophet ﷺ went forward to greet him and he rose up opening his great wings until all Heaven and Earth were covered by them. He kissed the Prophet and announced that he had been sent with a very special gift. Allah was giving the Prophet ﷺ and his nation the sacred month of *Ramadan* during which the gates of Hell are closed and Heaven draws near the earth. All who fast in this blessed month are forgiven their mistakes and its blessing and benefits are without measure.

The Prophet ﷺ and Jibra'il ﷺ traveled on until they came to an open space where all that could be heard was the scratching sound of the Divine Pen (*Qalam*) writing. Here Jibra'il ﷺ stopped and told the Prophet ﷺ to go on ahead. They came to a veil of gold. Jibra'il ﷺ shook it and a voice questioned who was asking to pass through. Jibra'il ﷺ replied as before, "It is I, Jibra'il ﷺ, and with me is the Prophet Muhammad ﷺ." From within the veil a voice answered, "*Allahu Akbar*." The Prophet ﷺ asked Jibra'il ﷺ where they were and who the Angel was behind the veil. But Jibra'il ﷺ had never gone this far before. He knew neither the place nor the Angel. His station was the *Sidrat ul-Muntaha* and he had only been allowed to pass farther in order to keep company with the Prophet ﷺ. Now the Prophet ﷺ must proceed alone.

The angel behind the veil then stretched out his hand and in the blink of an eye he pulled the Prophet ﷺ through to the other side. He directed the Prophet ﷺ to move ahead of him until they came to a veil of pearl. Here the same thing happened. He was carried to the other side by an angel showing him great respect and honor. In this way he passed through seventy thousand veils, each made of a different precious jewel, until he came to the other side where he found himself all alone.

Something came towards him. It looked like a green footstool or cushion flying through the air. Its name is the *Rafraf*. It spoke to the Prophet ﷺ greeting him and inviting him to sit upon it. Then it traveled through space until it arrived at the *Kursi*. The *Kursi* is made of pearls and is like the courtyard before the throne. If all the Seven Heavens and Seven Earths were spread out on the *Kursi* they would be as a child's ring lost in the desert.

Between the *Kursi* and the *'Arsh* there are seventy veils. The Prophet ﷺ passed through these veils one by one. Behind each one he saw empty thrones covered in silks and jewels. He asked the guardians of these seats to whom they belonged, what highly ranked prophets would occupy such honored places. The guardians replied that these thrones waited for the souls of two kinds of people from among the followers of Muhammad ﷺ. Those thrones, set close to the Divine Throne, were intended for those who memorize Quran, understand it and act on their understanding, and for those who get out of their comfortable beds in the middle of the night while the rest of the world sleeps in order to worship their Lord.

The Prophet ﷺ saw numberless strange seas and unusual and wondrous creatures in his journey through the seventy veils. He saw huge and frightening angels of all shapes and sizes. He could not even form the words to tell us all that he saw.

Then he reached to the Divine Throne, the *'Arsh*. It is made of green emeralds and has four legs of ruby. One Angel holds up each of the legs until the Judgment Day when four more Angels will join them, making eight in all. The first Angel has the form of a man who prays for the welfare of mankind. The second Angel has the form of an eagle and he prays for the welfare of the birds. The third Angel has the form of a lion and he prays for the welfare of the beasts of prey. The fourth Angel has the form of an ox and he prays for the welfare of the domestic animals. Compared to the *'Arsh*, the *Kursi* and the Seven Heavens and Earths are as a single candle hanging from a sky full of stars. Circling around the *'Arsh* are seventy thousand rows of angels reciting "*Allahu Akbar*" and "*La ilaha ill'Allah*". Written on the rim of the *'Arsh* is the phrase:

La ilaha ill'Allah Muhammadur Rasulullah

When the Prophet ﷺ reached the Divine Throne a drop of moisture rolled off it into his mouth. Its sweetness was incomparable. It filled his heart with the knowledge and wisdom of all that had gone before and was yet to come. The light from the Throne blazed around him until he was aware of nothing but that light. He saw everything there was to see with the eye of his heart.

He could see behind him as clearly as he could see before him. Nothing was hidden from him. The secrets of the world were visible to him.

After this, all became quiet. He heard no sound, no noise of any kind. In this vast, absolute silence he began to feel great fear. Just then Allah, in Loving Kindness, spoke to him in the voice of his friend Abu Bakr ﷺ. The sound of a familiar, friendly voice in a place otherwise so vast and strange gave the Prophet ﷺ comfort, and the terror left his heart.

14

The Divine Presence

The Prophet ﷺ now approached the Divine Throne. Before we continue we must pause in our story to make sure some things are quite clear. The Prophet ﷺ was not raised to this high place in order to actually see Allah Almighty. Allah cannot be seen like created things can be seen. He cannot be contained in any particular place, not even on His Throne. He cannot be contained in any particular form, whether human, angelic or any other. He cannot even be contained in any particular time period, day, hour or second. Whatever you can imagine, Allah is Greater than that. Allah is the Greatest, *Allahu Akbar,* which is what the angels of the seventy veils were chanting. The Prophet ﷺ was invited on this journey in order to see and experience the signs of Allah's creation, all of which were being shown to him. None of the things he then told to us are exaggerated. In order to help us to understand, some things may have been described as similar to other things with which we are familiar. But the greatness, the immensity, the wonder and strangeness of Allah's creations are totally beyond anything we can ever imagine. So we must try to open the eyes of our heart even a little in order to see with them what these poor words are trying to say.

When he reached the Divine Throne, the Prophet Muhammad ﷺ began to remove his sandals as we do when we enter a mosque. But the Throne itself spoke to him, telling him to please leave them on. The Throne was hoping for the honor of wiping the dust from the sandals of Allah's Beloved.

Then Allah Almighty spoke and ordered the Prophet Muhammad ﷺ to look around him. He saw a great sea with no end in sight. On its near shore a tree was growing, and on a branch of that tree sat a dove. In its beak the dove held a pebble the size of a lentil. The Lord told the

Prophet ﷺ that the tree is like the world, the dove is the Muslim nation, and the pebble is like the sins of that nation. The endless sea is the Ocean of Allah's Mercy into which the pebble will fall and dissolve into nothing. The joy of the noble Prophet ﷺ knew no bounds.

Then Allah said, "Come near to Me, O best of mankind. Come close, O Ahmad ﷺ, O Muhammad ﷺ, so that the Friend may be in intimate association with His friend." Then the blessed Prophet ﷺ was given a vision of the Divine Face of Beauty that is beyond all space and time, free from all conditions and all qualities, the One from Whom all else descends.

When he was face to face with the Divine Beauty he was inspired to say:
At-tahiyyatu lillahi was-salawatu wat-tayyibatu.
"Greetings to Allah and glory to Him. All worship and all good works belong to Him." The Lord Almighty answered him:
As-salamu 'alayka ayyuhan nabiyyu wa rahmatullahi
wa barakatuhu.
"Greetings to you, O Prophet, and the Mercy and Blessings of Allah upon you." The Prophet ﷺ then responded:
As-salamu 'alayna wa 'ala 'ibadillahis salihin.
"Peace be upon all of us and the righteous servants of Allah." Jibra'il ﷺ heard this conversation between Allah and His Beloved Muhammad ﷺ from where he sat on his branch of the *Sidrat ul-Muntaha*. He was moved to say:
Ash-hadu an la ilaha ill'Allah,
wa ash-hadu anna Muhammadan 'abduhu wa rasuluhu.
"I bear witness that there is no god but Allah and I bear witness that Muhammad is His servant and messenger." We repeat this conversation in memory of this blessed event whenever we sit in *qa'da* in every prayer we pray.

Muhammad ﷺ then asked what a person can do to erase any mistakes he may have made knowingly or unknowingly. He was told that if on a cold day he makes his *wudu'* in cold water, or if he goes out of his way to join in a prayer with others, or if when one prayer is finished he prepares for and looks forward to the next prayer, then he will end his life as pure and clean as he began it.

Allah then asked His Prophet ﷺ if he knew what actions lead to achieving a high station in Paradise? The Prophet ﷺ answered, "To share food with others and give them hospitality, to give *salams* to Muslims passing in the road whether you know them or not, and to rise for prayer at night when everyone else is asleep."

The Holy Prophet ﷺ reached a place of nearness and was given a vision of Divine Beauty. From the station of knowledge about certainty he passed to the station of the witnessing of certainty. Although before this the Prophet ﷺ had believed completely in what Allah told him even though he could not see it himself, now he believed in what his Lord said and he also saw it with his own eyes. Allah confirmed it at this time by giving him a new verse of Quran (2:285):

> *The messenger believes in what was sent down to him*
> *from his Lord.*

Muhammad ﷺ replied to this that yes, he truly did. Then Allah asked him who else believes. He replied:

> *And the believers; each one believes in God.*

Allah then asked in what else they believe. Muhammad ﷺ replied;

> *And His angels, and His books and His messengers.*
> *We make no distinction between any of His messengers.*

Allah then asked what the believers say when Allah's words are recited to them. He answered that they say:

> *We hear and we obey.*

The Lord Almighty answered that all this was truly spoken. He then asked if there was anything the Prophet ﷺ wished to ask for. Muhammad ﷺ said:

> *O Lord give us Your forgiveness, to You is*
> *the final homecoming,*

and with these words completed this most beautiful verse. Thereupon the Lord of Majesty replied that he had forgiven Muhammad ﷺ and those who love him. Allah then declared in words that begin the next verse in the Quran (2:286):

Allah burdens no soul with more than it can carry,
for it what it earns and against it what it has earned.

Again Allah permitted His Prophet ﷺ to ask for whatever he wished. Muhammad ﷺ asked:

Our Lord do not punish us for those things we have done
or for those things we have left undone.

When this was granted he asked:

Our Lord do not lay on us as heavy a burden as
You laid on those before us,

because the laws of the previous prophets were very strict and difficult to follow. Then the Prophet ﷺ asked:

Our Lord do not lay on us difficulties beyond our
strength to endure.

Then Muhammad ﷺ said:

Pardon us, forgive us, have mercy on us.

Allah granted the Prophet's ﷺ wishes. He pardoned him and his nation, and forgave him and his nation, and He granted mercy to him and his nation. Then the Holy Prophet ﷺ said:

You are our Protector. Help us against those who
do not believe,

and with these words completed the final verse of *Surat ul-Baqara*. Allah replied that He would be the Friend and Protector of the Muslims, in life and after death, forever.

Then Allah in His Great Generosity took the opening verses of the Quran, called *al-Fatiha* (The Opening), and the closing verses of its second chapter, *al-Baqara,* from the golden treasure chests next to the Divine Throne and gave them to the Prophet ﷺ. He told him that his mission would be different from that of any of the other prophets. He was being sent to the whole world, not just a small portion of it, and a symbol of this would be that the whole surface of the Earth

would be his prayer carpet, not just the mosque, church or temple. A Muslim can pray anywhere it is clean.

Then Allah Almighty taught Muhammad ﷺ some very important things to tell his nation. He said to teach them:

1) Love your Lord Who made you and continues to care for you and bless you.
2) Fear your Lord, if you fear anything, because He holds all power over you.
3) Ask your Lord directly for whatever you want because He is the Possessor of all things and the Most Generous.
4) Obey your Lord because His Commands are based on complete Knowledge and Understanding.

Then Muhammad ﷺ had a private conversation with his Lord that he did not share with us. As he was leaving he was told that his nation would be required to pray fifty prayers every day, fast for six months out of the year, and wash their clothes seven times before they would be considered clean. He accepted and began his return journey.

Paradise

The Lord offered the Prophet ﷺ a tour of the paradise gardens that were prepared for the believers. The *Rafraf* returned to pick him up and bring him to the *Sidrat ul-Muntaha* where Jibra'il ﷺ waited to accompany him to Paradise.

The gates of Paradise are made of red gold. They have five hundred columns of pearl, topaz, ruby, and emerald. In the middle of each is a ring containing forty thousand cities each with forty thousand domes within each of which dwell forty thousand angels. Each of these angels holds two trays of heavenly clothing and necklaces of light with which they will dress the souls as they enter.

Jibra'il ﷺ knocked at the gate and Ridwan ﷺ, its guardian Angel, answered. Jibra'il ﷺ said, "It is I, Jibra'il ﷺ, and with me is the Prophet Muhammad ﷺ." Ridwan ﷺ opened the gates. They saw him seated on a carved throne surrounded by angels who all rose to welcome Muhammad ﷺ with great joy. In front of the throne were a great many keys. Ridwan ﷺ said that whenever a person says, "*La ilaha ill'Allah*," the Almighty Lord creates for him a mansion in Paradise. The key to that mansion is given to Ridwan ﷺ for safekeeping until the soul of the owner arrives to claim it.

Ridwan ﷺ showed the Prophet ﷺ eight different paradise gardens. Four of these are actual gardens with orchards. They are named, *Firdaus, Ma'wa, 'Adn* and *Na'im*. Their walls are made of bricks of alternating gold, silver, ruby, chrysolite and pearl. The mortar used to cement them together is of musk and camphor. Yet this wall appeared clear as glass and through it the Prophet ﷺ could see laid out before him all the layers of Earths and Heavens leading up to the Divine Throne. The soil in the gardens is of musk and amber out of which grass grows bright yellow and purple and even the lowly pebbles and rocks are precious stones

There are four rivers that flow through all the gardens of Paradise, one of water, one of milk, one of wine that does not cause drunkenness, and one of honey. There are three springs, *Rahiq, Salsabil,* and *Tasnim.* The banks of the rivers are of gold set with pearls or of silver set with rubies. Gems of many colors sparkle from the riverbed that is visible through the clear, flowing water. Hyacinths and saffron crocuses grow up from the jeweled banks of the springs.

The trees in the gardens are so large that a man on horseback could ride seventy thousand years without leaving the shade cast by one of them. The roots of these trees are gold, their branches ruby, pearl and chrysolite. Their leaves look to be of silk, brocade and velvet. Each fruit is the size of a water jar and has seventy different delicious flavors. When one of the residents of Paradise is hungry a fruit falls, 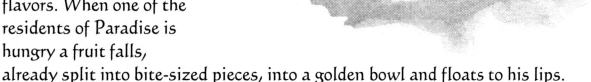 already split into bite-sized pieces, into a golden bowl and floats to his lips.

There are many birds with necks like camels and feathers in all the colors of Paradise. They sing beautifully and no one knows if their song or their appearance is more beautiful. When a resident of Paradise is hungry a bird will fall from the sky already roasted on a platter of gold. The meat is more delicious than any other. After he has been eaten he rises alive again from the bones and flies away singing, happy to have been enjoyed.

There are four more levels of Paradise, making eight in all. The fifth is named *Dar us-Salam*. The sixth is *Dar ul-Jalal*. The seventh is *Dar ul-Qarar* and the eighth is *Dar ul-Khuld*. Their gardens contain huge palaces and pavilions. The sky of the Highest Paradise is at the base of the Divine Throne.

The Prophet ﷺ was given a tour of the mansions of *'Adn*. Many of these were to belong to his companions and those who would follow them. Some of these were made of rubies with domes of pearl. Some were of multicolored gems

with domes of emerald, while others were of gold with domes of garnets. Every one of the seventy thousand rooms in each mansion holds a throne platform covered with a canopy and carpeted with downy pillows of embroidered silk to lie upon.

He saw one mansion larger than the rest and was told that it belonged to Abu Bakr as-Siddiq ﷺ. When he returned and gave Abu Bakr ﷺ the good news of his heavenly mansion, Abu Bakr ﷺ did not care about its beauty so long as it was near the Prophet ﷺ. He also saw the mansions of 'Umar ﷺ and 'Uthman ﷺ in *'Adn*. The mansion of 'Ali ﷺ was in the Paradise called *Na'im*.

At one point the Prophet ﷺ heard the footsteps of Bilal ﷺ up ahead of him. Later he asked Bilal ﷺ what he had done to receive such a high station. Bilal ﷺ thought hard and finally said that maybe it was because each time he renewed his *wudu'* he prayed two *rak'as*.

The Prophet ﷺ saw two mansions belonging to Zayd ibn 'Amr ibn Nufayl ﷺ. Zayd ﷺ was a good Christian before accepting the Prophet ﷺ and becoming a good Muslim. Therefore Allah had rewarded him with two mansions. He also saw the mansion belonging to Ghamsa bint Milhan ﷺ, a poor woman who was very patient and never complained. He saw his wife Khadija ﷺ in a pavilion of pearls built on the banks of one of the rivers of Paradise.

The Prophet ﷺ saw a tree that was even more beautiful and enormous than the others. This tree is called *Tuba*, the Tree of Repentance. It is very beautiful and has the best scent of anything in all the paradise gardens. Its fruits are like long tubes and they taste like all the delicious things on Earth and in the Heavens all rolled into one.

Of all the beautiful and amazing things the rivers of Paradise were the most interesting to the Prophet ﷺ. He asked Jibra'il ﷺ about them. He wanted to know where they came from and to where they were flowing. Jibra'il ﷺ himself did not know, so Allah sent a large Angel to answer the Prophet's ﷺ

question. This Angel lowered one of his many great wings and asked the Prophet ﷺ to step on and then close his eyes. They flew off and after some time the Angel asked him to open his eyes again.

The Prophet ﷺ saw a tree growing out of a dome so big that if the whole world were placed upon that dome it would look like a small sparrow perched on a towering mountain. The Angel instructed the Prophet ﷺ to open the green door in the dome. When he tried he found the door locked. The Angel than told him that the words, "*Bismillahir Rahmanir Rahim*," were the key to open that door. The Prophet ﷺ repeated this phrase and the door sprang open.

Inside he saw the four rivers each flowing from one of the four walls of the great building supporting the dome. On one wall was written, "*Bismi*," and from the letter *mim* flowed the river of water. On another wall was written "*Allah*," and from the letter *ha* flowed the river of milk. On the third wall was written "*ar-Rahman*" and out of that *mim* flowed the river of wine. On the fourth wall was written "*ar-Rahim*" and from its *mim* flowed the river of honey. In this way the Prophet ﷺ understood that the source of the waters of Paradise is this wonderful phrase, "In the Name of Allah, the Kind and the Caring."

Whoever speaks these words, "*Bismillahir Rahmanir Rahim*," with a pure heart will drink from the rivers of Paradise.

Then the Prophet ﷺ and Jibra'il ﷺ began to retrace their steps down through the Seven Heavens. In the Seventh Heaven they saw Ibrahim ﷺ who congratulated the Prophet ﷺ on his ascension (*Mi'raj*). In the Sixth Heaven they saw Musa ﷺ who congratulated him also but asked him what obligations Allah Almighty had given for his nation. Muhammad ﷺ replied that they were required to pray fifty times each day and fast six months of the year, and wash their clothes seven times to make them clean. Musa ﷺ knew from his own experience that human beings are too weak to do all of this. He advised Muhammad ﷺ to return to Allah and plead with Him to reduce the obligations given to his weak nation.

The Prophet ﷺ turned around and retraced his steps to the *Sidrat ul-Muntaha*. He threw himself into *sajda* and prayed that Allah Almighty have mercy on his nation. The Merciful Lord reduced the prayers to forty times a day, the fasting to five months, and the washings to six. On returning to the Sixth Heaven, the Prophet ﷺ again met Musa ﷺ who advised him to return a second time as the burden of obligations remained too heavy.

Muhammad ﷺ returned to the *Sidrat ul-Muntaha*. Allah in His Kindness reduced the prayer to thirty times, the fast to four months and the washing to five. On hearing this Musa ﷺ was still not satisfied. Muhammad ﷺ returned to plead with Allah yet a third time. The prayer was again reduced, to twenty times a day. Fasting was reduced to three months and laundering to four times. Still Musa ﷺ advised that the burden would be too great. Muhammad ﷺ returned again and again. For our sake he continued to beg his Lord until only five prayers a day remained, and one month of fasting and one washing to

purify clothes. Musa ﷺ thought it was still too heavy a burden, but Muhammad ﷺ was too embarrassed to return to Allah another time.

As Muhammad ﷺ was departing from the Sixth Heaven he heard the Divine Voice. As His final gift to the Prophet ﷺ Allah said that if the Muslims pray five prayers a day He will count it as if they had prayed all fifty. In addition, any good deed a Muslim performs Allah will reward it as if he had done ten good deeds. Any good deed a Muslim plans to do but does not actually accomplish Allah will reward as if it were done. And if he even thinks to do something bad and then does not, Allah will reward him as if he had done a good deed. All thanks are due to Allah Who gives beyond even our ability to ask and beyond our ability to measure.

After this Jibra'il ﷺ and the Prophet Muhammad ﷺ climbed down through all the Heavens until they reached the Earth. There they saw the city of Jerusalem spread out before them and the *Buraq* ﷺ still tied to its tether ring where they had left it. The Prophet ﷺ prayed two *rak'as* thanking Allah Almighty for His Infinite Mercy and Generosity. He mounted the *Buraq* ﷺ and returned in the blink of an eye to the house of Umm Hani ﷺ in Mecca. When he arrived he found that the rug in the courtyard was still warm from where he had been sleeping upon it. As we measure time, he had only been gone for less than three hours.

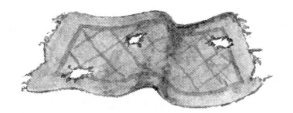

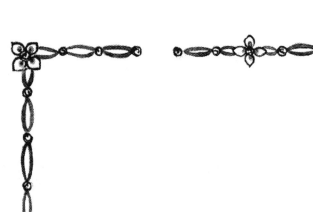

16

The Pledge at 'Aqaba

The next morning the Prophet ﷺ went to the Ka'aba to pray. There he met with some of the unbelievers who, seeing his face shining like the moon, asked him what had happened during the night. He answered truthfully that he had visited the *Bayt ul-Maqdis* in Jerusalem and journeyed to the Seven Heavens. The people of Mecca were traders. They knew quite well that it took at least a month of walking to travel the distance between Mecca and Jerusalem. They began to laugh at the noble Prophet ﷺ and called him a liar.

They gathered their friends and neighbors, telling them that this Muhammad ﷺ, who imagined that God spoke to him, now also imagined that he could fly through the air and visit faraway places and return in one night before anyone even knew he was gone.

A crowd gathered and it was not a nice crowd. Sadly, even some of the believers began to feel doubts. This was such an unusual event that a few began to wonder if maybe Muhammad ﷺ really was a little crazy. Many more of the Muslims wondered if maybe the Prophet ﷺ meant that he had made this journey in his dreams. But Muhammad ﷺ had traveled awake and in his body. He said so and we believe him.

When the news reached Abu Bakr ﷺ he was surprised and asked the people if they had actually heard the Prophet ﷺ say with his own words that he had traveled to Jerusalem and the Seven Heavens in one night. They answered that in fact they had heard him. "Then," said Abu Bakr ﷺ, "he did just exactly what he said." There was not one speck of doubt in his heart. The Muslims questioned him again asking him how he thought such a thing was physically possible. Abu Bakr ﷺ replied that they had believed the Prophet ﷺ before when he said he spoke to angels and heard the words of Allah. Why was this news so much harder to believe? Abu Bakr ﷺ, without hesitation, told them clearly that he believed every word the Prophet ﷺ had said. From this day on he was called Abu Bakr as-Siddiq ﷺ, a title meaning the one who supports the Truth, because he accepted without the slightest doubt the miracle of the *Mi'raj*.

The unbelievers gathered around the Prophet ﷺ and began to question him. Some of them had been to Jerusalem and knew the city well. They began to ask him of its landmarks, streets and shops. In fact, the Prophet ﷺ had been too absorbed in his Lord and the angels and prophets to look around him at the scenery. But Allah gave a vision to the Prophet ﷺ of the city of Jerusalem spread out before him like a map. He only had to look to answer each question put to him with complete accuracy, down to details even the questioners had forgotten.

Then the Prophet ﷺ told them of a caravan on its way to Mecca that was still several days journey away. He had seen it when he flew over on the *Buraq* ﷺ. The caravan arrived in a few days just as he had said it would.

This miraculous event and its many proofs did convince some people, but unbelievably the majority of the people still refused to believe. They remained as if they were deaf, blind and with hearts of stone. Nothing the Prophet ﷺ said or did was enough for them. May Allah protect us from ever

being anything like them. We believe in all the wonderful things the Prophet ﷺ has told us.

Instead of making things better for the Muslims in Mecca, the *Mi'raj* of the Prophet ﷺ only seemed to make things worse. However, Mecca was not the only place to hear of the Prophet's ﷺ message. People from all over the area journeyed to Mecca to buy and sell and to worship the strange statues in the Ka'aba. At these markets the Muslims spoke to whoever would listen. Many of these visitors became Muslim and went back to their villages or bedouin encampments to tell their families and friends the good news. So even while Mecca remained openly hostile to the Prophet ﷺ, Islam was beginning to spread beyond the borders of Mecca. In this way six men of Yathrib, the village of the Prophet's ﷺ mother, came to Mecca to trade and got something more valuable then they could ever have imagined.

Yathrib is six days journey north of Mecca. It is an oasis with groves of date palms, springs and fertile land. The people there were farmers belonging to two Arab tribes, the Aws and the Khazraj. In addition three Jewish tribes lived in fortified villages outside of town. None of these tribes got along very well. They had just succeeded in making a fragile peace after a long civil war in which even the Jewish tribes had taken sides and fought. Usually, however, the Jewish tribes opposed the Arab tribes and would tell them that they waited only for their prophet to come to lead them to victory. They expected this prophet to come from their own people. At his coming they would unite and together destroy the Arabs.

When the six men of Khazraj first met the Prophet ﷺ they thought to themselves that he must be the one of whom the Jews had spoken. They were afraid to wait and let the other tribes find him first so they wasted no time in accepting him. They returned to Yathrib and told their people about Islam. Many listened, some became Muslim.

The next year five of the six returned bringing with them seven of their friends to make twelve in all. It was the time of the big market and pilgrimage in Mecca and they arranged to meet the Prophet ﷺ in secret at a place called 'Aqaba. All twelve accepted Islam and pledged themselves to the Prophet ﷺ. They made him a sacred promise that they would believe in Allah, the One God, and associate nothing else with Him. They promised not to steal or do anything indecent. They promised not to kill any of their children. At that time it was not uncommon for parents to kill the babies they felt they were unable to feed or care for. They did not understand that Allah is the Provider. He gives food and life to all His creation. A child born into this world arrives with its provision already written for it. Allah will care for it and feed it, as He knows best. They also promised the Prophet ﷺ not to tell lies intended to hurt anyone, and they vowed to obey the Prophet ﷺ in whatever he advised them.

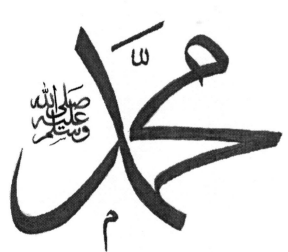

After this the Prophet ﷺ sent them home to Yathrib with one of the Qurayshi Muslims, Mus'ab ibn Umayr ﷺ. He would be their *imam* and teach them Quran. The Aws would not follow a man of Khazraj nor would the Khazraj follow a man of Aws. They needed an *imam* who came from neither tribe. Many people of Yathrib became Muslim at the hands of Mus'ab ﷺ. Powerful and poor alike accepted Islam until almost every family of Aws and Khazraj had Muslims among them.

The next year, when the time of the big market and pilgrimage came again, Mus'ab ﷺ returned to Mecca. He brought with him seventy of the nobles of both Aws and Khazraj and also two women. The Prophet ﷺ was sitting on a rug in the shade of the Ka'aba with his uncle 'Abbas ﷺ. The men of Yathrib, most of whom had never before even met Muhammad ﷺ, approached him slowly with their eyes cast down in respect. In front of all the unkind and suspicious stares of the men of Mecca, the seventy from Yathrib asked to take the same oath that their friends had taken the year before. In addition, they

asked that the Prophet ﷺ come back with them to Yathrib and be their leader to unite them and keep the peace.

The Prophet ﷺ agreed to meet with them later at 'Aqaba where they had met the year before. The Prophet's ﷺ uncle, 'Abbas ﵁, asked to go with him because he was worried about what he had heard. Although he had not yet become Muslim himself, 'Abbas ﵁ was still protective of his nephew, Muhammad ﷺ. He spoke to the nobles of Yathrib, telling them that if they took Muhammad ﷺ from his family in Mecca they must be sure that they were able and ready to protect him. Come what may, they must be willing to defend Muhammad ﷺ; otherwise it would be better for them all if he remained in Mecca where he still had close family who, out of family honor, would continue to protect him.

The people of Yathrib added to their pledge to protect Muhammad ﷺ with their lives. One by one they took his hand and promised that whatever came they would follow, obey and defend him. The Prophet ﷺ also pledged himself to them, to guide them, to teach them and to be one of them. He said to them, "You are mine and I am yours."

The Prophet ﷺ had finally found a safe home for the Muslims. He gave the order for the Muslims of Mecca to leave for Yathrib. He counseled them to migrate one by one, quietly so as not to attract attention, over the next few months. When all of them had safely gone the Prophet ﷺ himself promised to follow.

The Prophet ﷺ was sent as a light for all the world. But just as a lamp that brightens the whole room leaves a shadow at its base, so the light of the Prophet ﷺ was not visible to many of those in the city of his birth. With his move to Yathrib maybe, at last, they would come out of the darkness of the shadow.

17

The Hijra

As the Muslims fled in small groups from Mecca to Yathrib, the Quraysh began to notice their absence. They worried that if Muhammad ﷺ were to leave he would begin to collect enough followers to form an army and return to attack Mecca itself. They thought it was a matter of tribal security, of their very survival. They decided to kill Muhammad ﷺ and finally end this threat, once and for all. The problem in doing this was that his family and their allies would take revenge on the murderer and his family who would then be obliged to retaliate. It would start a civil war among the Quraysh and a blood feud that could last for years.

While they were discussing what to do, the accursed *Shaytan* took human form and entered among the group. He spurred them on to kill Muhammad ﷺ, saying it was the only real solution. He suggested that if a representative from each family of Quraysh acted together it would involve the entire tribe and so the family of Muhammad ﷺ would be unable to take revenge on all of them. It was decided that they would take care of their problem that very night.

Meanwhile Jibra'il ﷺ appeared to the Prophet ﷺ and told him to get ready, for the time to flee had arrived. The Holy Prophet ﷺ called 'Ali ﷺ to him and asked him to cover himself with the Prophet's ﷺ cloak and spend that night in the Prophet's ﷺ bed. In this way the unbelievers would think the Prophet ﷺ asleep in his bed when in reality he

would be making his escape. He told 'Ali ؇ not to fear for Allah would protect him and that later he could join the Prophet ؙ in Yathrib.

The Prophet ؙ then went to Abu Bakr ؇ who had been waiting and hoping for just such a moment. They agreed to meet at midnight and go to a cave on the mountain of Thawr. Abu Bakr's ؇ daughter, Asma ؇, would sneak 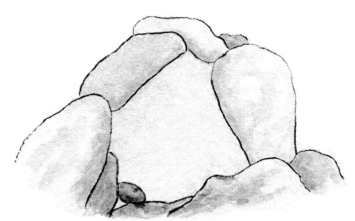 them food and water. They would hide there for three days and then a servant of Abu Bakr ؇ would bring them two fine camels kept in readiness and a guide who would lead them across the desert to Yathrib.

The Prophet ؙ went home and waited. The Quraysh, led by Abu Jahl, the enemy of God, took up their hiding places outside the door. When the Prophet ؙ emerged in the morning they intended for each one to stab him with his knife. 'Ali ؇ wrapped himself in the Prophet's ؙ cloak and lay down without fear or hesitation on the Prophet's ؙ bed. He would gladly have given his life to save Muhammad ؙ but he was confident of Allah's protection. That night Allah sent His angels to stand guard over 'Ali ؇ where he slept.

The Prophet ؙ began reciting *Surat Yasin* up to the verse that says:
>*And We have put before them a barrier, and behind them a barrier; and We have covered them, so they do not see.* (36:7)

The Prophet ؙ opened his door and walked right past the unbelievers, but they saw nothing. He met up with Abu Bakr ؇ and the two of them walked quickly to the cave on the mountain of Thawr. As they walked Abu Bakr ؇ blurred their footprints so no one would be able to track them.

In the morning, through the window, the unbelievers saw 'Ali ؇ rise from the Prophet's ؙ bed. They were furious that they had been tricked and had missed their opportunity. They went immediately to the house of Abu Bakr ؇ and knocked. Asma ؇ answered and bravely denied that she had any knowledge

of the whereabouts of her father. Abu Jahl hit her in the face so hard that her earring flew off, but she told them nothing. For the next three nights that courageous girl went alone in the dead of night through the streets with the enemy surrounding her, up the dark mountain to bring food, water, and news to her father and the Prophet ﷺ.

The Quraysh searched high and low for the fugitives. Abu Bakr ؓ and the Prophet ﷺ hid in the back of the cave. They heard the search party coming closer. A spider began to spin her web over the mouth of the cave. They watched her spin faster than any spider they had ever seen. A rock dove made her nest next to the web in the entrance and she laid three eggs. Then a wind arose and blew sand until it laid a fine layer of dust over everything. It looked as if it had been there undisturbed for a hundred years. Jibra'il ؈ came to see if they were safe and laughed at the little spider spinning her fragile web. The spider said, "Don't laugh at me. I am spinning on the Command of my Lord. This is not an ordinary web." Jibra'il ؈ tried to tear it but, try as he might, he could not snap a single thread of its silk.

The search party came right up to the mouth of the cave. Abu Bakr ؓ could see their feet through the opening. He began to fear that they would be discovered and that something would happen to his beloved friend. Muhammad ﷺ consoled him by reminding him that if two believers are together then Allah is the third with them. He recited a verse of Quran:

> If you do not help him yet Allah has helped him already.
> When the unbelievers drove him away the second of two, when the two were in the cave, when he said to his companion, "Sorrow not, surely Allah is with us." Then Allah sent down on him His Peace and strengthened him with legions you did not see. (9:40)

Abu Bakr's ﷺ heart became calm and they heard the unbelievers say that no one could have entered that cave without ripping the web or disturbing the dove. Even *Shaytan*, who was with them, looked inside the cave and saw nothing. The search party went on its way, blind and deaf as always.

The Prophet ﷺ was tired. Abu Bakr ﷺ said he would stay awake and keep watch while the Prophet ﷺ got some sleep. He laid his blessed head on Abu Bakr's ﷺ knee and slept while Abu Bakr ﷺ quietly recited Quran. All of a sudden Abu Bakr ﷺ saw a snake raise its head from a hole in the cave floor. He

quickly stuffed his cloak into the hole to keep the snake from coming out. But the snake began to come out another hole nearby. Abu Bakr ﷺ had nothing left with which to block the second hole so he placed the heel of his foot securely into it. The snake bit him hard and deep. Abu Bakr ﷺ was afraid to move for he did not want to

wake the Prophet ﷺ. But the pain was so great that tears welled up in his eyes and one fell on the Prophet's ﷺ blessed cheek.

The Prophet ﷺ woke quickly and saw the snake. He scolded him for biting his friend and causing him pain. The snake was given human speech and he defended himself saying that four hundred and fifty years earlier he had heard the word of 'Isa ﷺ telling about the coming of the Last Prophet named Ahmad ﷺ. The snake had been waiting all this time just to catch a glimpse of this beloved Prophet ﷺ. Now, just as he was going to achieve his heart's desire, Abu Bakr ﷺ put his foot in the hole and blocked the snake's view. The snake said he was sorry but he had had to bite Abu Bakr ﷺ. The Prophet ﷺ sucked the poison from Abu Bakr's ﷺ wound and spit it out at the entrance to the cave. From his spit a wild rose grew, with green leaves and thorns from the poison, white flowers from the Prophet's ﷺ saliva and red berries (rosehips) from Abu Bakr's ﷺ blood.

Then the Prophet ﷺ smiled at the snake and stroked him. The snake was the color of saffron and, at the touch of the Prophet ﷺ, it gave off a delightful

scent. The Prophet ﷺ made it promise that it would never again hurt anyone of his nation. There are many of these snakes that still live in the hills of Mecca. They still give off a wonderful smell and no one hurts them and they harm no one.

On the morning of the fourth day, which was a Thursday the first of *Rabi' ul-Awwal,* the servant brought the camels and the Bedouin guide. They set out on their journey. The Prophet ﷺ looked back at his beloved homeland. As the city of his birth and the Ka'aba receded into the distance he felt great sadness that he might never see them again. But Allah Almighty reassured him that one day he would return in triumph.

Because Quraysh were looking for them everywhere, they took an indirect route. First they went west to the sea before heading north. The Quraysh had offered a reward to anyone who found them, so when they saw a Bedouin rider they became alarmed. His name was Suraqa ﷺ and he was a brave warrior and a bounty hunter. He rode towards them already counting his reward money. Just then Jibra'il ﷺ announced to the Prophet ﷺ that the Lord had put the earth at his command. The Prophet ﷺ ordered the earth to swallow Suraqa ﷺ. Suraqa ﷺ began to sink as if he were in quicksand. When he promised to let the Prophet ﷺ go free, the Prophet ﷺ commanded the earth to let Suraqa ﷺ go. Three times he broke his word and threatened to capture the Prophet ﷺ. Three times the earth swallowed his legs to the knees until he relented. After the third try he was finally convinced and let them continue on their way without trouble. He kept silent about all that he had seen. Eight years later he became Muslim and finally told his story.

18

The Entry Into Medina

The people of Yathrib had heard the news that the Prophet ﷺ had escaped from Mecca. They eagerly awaited his arrival, but days passed and he still had not come. Of course, they did not know that he had spent three days in the cave and then had taken a long and indirect route. Every morning at dawn some of the men in the outlying oasis of Quba went out onto the wide lava fields that bordered the settlement to look  for him. One morning they saw white specks against the black field and knew that the ones they were hoping for had come.

At noon, on a Monday, the twelfth of the month of *Rabi' ul-Awwal,* the day of the Prophet's ﷺ birth, Muhammad ﷺ and Abu Bakr ؓ rode into Quba. The light that shone from their faces outshone the midday sun. All the Muslims came out to greet them. They were exhausted from their long ordeal so they stayed to rest in Quba for two weeks. During this time the first mosque was built and named *Masjid at-Taqwa.* On Friday, the Holy Prophet ﷺ prayed *Juma'a* openly with one hundred Muslims following him. It was Islam's first *Juma'a* prayer and first *khutba.*

When the *Juma'a* prayer was done the Prophet ﷺ mounted his camel, Qaswa, and prepared to enter Yathrib. After years of being persecuted only for speaking the Truth, the Prophet ﷺ rode out in the open with dignity and honor surrounded by the love and respect that he deserved. The whole Muslim population of Yathrib accompanied the Prophet ﷺ into the city. The Muslim men of Aws and Khazraj rode in two lines on either side of him with their swords drawn, to demonstrate to all men and *Jinn* their willingness to give their lives for him. The women and children followed behind singing a song of welcome they had composed especially for the Prophet ﷺ. It is called *Tala'al badru 'alayna*. Maybe you know it because the whole Muslim world still sings it today to welcome the beloved Prophet ﷺ into their hearts. That Friday, the Muslims of Yathrib welcomed the Prophet ﷺ into their homes and into their hearts. They sang:

> The full moon (the Prophet ﷺ) has risen over us.
> From the valley of *Wada'*
> We owe it to show gratefulness
> For the one who calls us to Allah.
>
> Oh you who are sent among us,
> You come with a command that must be obeyed.
> You have brought honor and nobleness to our city.
> Welcome to you, O best of callers to Allah.

From this point on, Yathrib was referred to by a new name of great honor for which it is much better known. It was renamed *Madinat un-Nabi*, the City of the Prophet ﷺ, or Medina for short. Even though it was in the heat of the day, the entire population of Medina lined the road to greet the Prophet ﷺ as he rode into their town. From the rooftops people watched the grand procession and shouted their welcome. Men stood in front of their doors and tried to catch hold of Qaswa's bridle to invite the Prophet ﷺ to stop and stay with them. The Prophet ﷺ smiled and blessed each one, but he asked them to let his camel go free because she was being guided by Allah and would stop at the spot He had chosen.

There was a man living in Medina named Abu Ayyub ﷺ. His great, great grandfather had been one of the kings of Yemen. This king worshipped idols

until one day he heard some Christians talking about a prophet who would be born in Arabia. The king conceived a desire to see this prophet. On learning that he was not expected for another hundred years, the king became very sad. The love in his heart grew and he determined to find a way to reach out into the future and somehow serve and receive the blessings of this prophet.

The king set out for Mecca with a caravan of precious gifts. He presented these at the Ka'aba, including the first cloth covering for the House itself. He was then guided to continue on to the small oasis of Yathrib. The king told his son and his son's wife who were traveling with him to build a house and stay in

Yathrib. He hoped that they would prosper and have children whose children would one day fulfill his most heartfelt desire to serve the expected prophet. The king left a sealed letter with his son begging the prophet of the last days to accept him as one of his nation and, on the Day of Judgment, to shelter him under the banner of his protection. The king wrapped his petition in layers of precious silk and put it inside a box

that he entrusted to the safekeeping of his son. Over the course of time the grandchildren of the king lost all their wealth and became quite poor. They continued to live and farm in the small village of Yathrib. They had not lost the box although they had forgotten what was in it.

On this day, the Prophet's ﷺ camel was being invisibly led by Jibra'il ﷺ. Abu Ayyub ؓ was hoping, like all the men of Medina, that the Prophet ﷺ would stop at his house, but he doubted there was any likelihood of its happening. He was poor and there were so many others, more wealthy and more powerful than he, who were competing to host the Prophet ﷺ. But Jibra'il ﷺ led Qaswa to the door of Abu Ayyub ؓ and there she knelt down. They prodded her until she stood up, but she knelt down again and refused to go further.

Abu Ayyub ﷺ and his wife began to cry tears of joy. They escorted the Prophet ﷺ into their humble house. They had two rooms, one above the other. The Prophet ﷺ asked for the ground floor because he said it would be easier for his many visitors to come and go without disturbing Abu Ayyub ﷺ and his family. That night, however, after the Prophet ﷺ lay down to sleep, Abu Ayyub ﷺ and his wife were unable to sleep. They were shy even to walk across the room to their bed for fear the floor would creak and wake the Prophet ﷺ. The idea of being above his head, between him and his Lord, also made them very uncomfortable. They spent the night huddled in the stairway. In the morning the Noble Prophet ﷺ agreed to move to the upstairs room so that his hosts could get some rest.

That morning the Prophet ﷺ asked Abu Ayyub ﷺ if he did not have something in safekeeping for him. Abu Ayyub ﷺ was puzzled. He could not think what it was. He was a poor man. He had nothing of value. The Prophet ﷺ

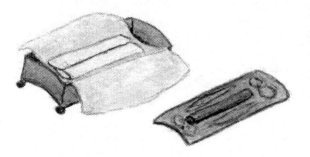

then had to remind him of the sealed box of his grandfather. Abu Ayyub ﷺ brought out the box from where it had been hidden and all but forgotten. The Prophet ﷺ unwrapped and read the letter. He accepted the wish of the long dead king. He prayed for him and for his grandson, Abu Ayyub ﷺ. He prayed that the Lord honor him in this world and the next.

Abu Ayyub ﷺ lived a long and blessed life. As an old man he accompanied the armies of Sultan Yazid to Constantinople. There he died a

martyr outside the walls of the city, and his tomb has become a beautiful mosque and place of pilgrimage for the Muslims of Asia Minor.

The Prophet ﷺ stayed a couple of months in the house of Abu Ayyub ؓ while his mosque and adjoining house were being built. Then his daughters were brought from Mecca and his wife, Sawda ؓ, whom he had married after the death of Khadija ؓ. 'Ali ؓ had already arrived and Abu Bakr's ؓ daughters, Asma ؓ and 'Aisha ؓ, and their mother, Umm Ruman ؓ, were soon to follow.

The men and women who left Mecca to accompany the Prophet ﷺ had abandoned everything familiar and safe. They had left their homes and families, their livelihoods and property. They arrived in Medina with nothing but what they could carry and their great love for Allah and His Prophet ﷺ. They are called *Muhajirin*, the emigrants, and Allah has blessed them and honored them above others for their sacrifices and their unfaltering devotion to His Way.

The *Muhajirin* were received in Medina by complete strangers who, only for love of Allah and His Prophet ﷺ, opened their hearts and their homes to them. Although the people of Medina were not wealthy they shared all they had with the emigrants from Mecca. The Prophet ﷺ paired them together, one man from Medina with one man from Mecca. They became like brothers. If a man had two rooms he gave one to his brother. If he had two dates he gave one to his brother. The people of Medina who opened their hearts to the *Muhajirin* were called the *Ansar,* the helpers. Allah has blessed them and honored them also above all others.

This journey from Mecca to Medina is called the *Hijra.* From it the Prophet ﷺ began counting the years of the Muslim calendar. It was a new beginning for the Muslims of Mecca and for the whole world. Something brand new was just getting started, a new era was dawning. This calendar is called the *Hijri* calendar. Just as the Christian calendar begins with the birth of 'Isa ﷺ and its years are designated CE, so the

Muslim calendar begins with the *Hijra* and its years are marked AH. 1 AH is the equivalent of 622 CE.

19

The Battle of Badr

The first year in Medina was not without its problems. The men of Aws and Khazraj had some difficulties getting used to being together and cooperating. Some of the chiefs of the tribes felt that their power and position had been diminished by the Prophet ﷺ, and they became jealous. Some of the tribes were suspicious of the new religion. The *Muhajirin* felt homesick and the Prophet ﷺ prayed that one day Medina would become as dear to them as their own city of Mecca. There were many adjustments to be made, but the first year brought with it exciting changes as well.

The *qibla* was changed. The Muslims were directed in a verse of Quran to pray facing the Holy Ka'aba in Mecca rather than the Holy House in Jerusalem, the direction they had turned for prayer until then. The first mosque in Quba had to be altered. Today it is called the *Masjid al-Qiblatain,* the mosque with the two *qiblas,* one facing north to Jerusalem and one facing south towards Mecca.

The Prophet's ﷺ mosque was completed with the new *qibla*. The *adhan,* or call to prayer, was perfected and instituted. Bilal ﷺ was designated the first *muadhdhin*. He climbed to the roof of the tallest house in Medina and announced the times of prayer with a beautiful voice. With no fear of retaliation or need for secrecy the

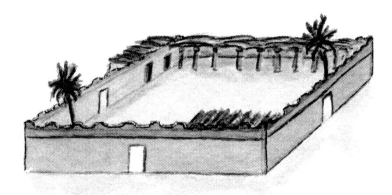

Muslims of Medina attended prayers at the mosque openly five times a day. Some of the prayers were now extended to four *rak'as,* whereas until then they had all consisted of only two. Ramadan was prescribed for the Muslims. They were ordered to begin fasting at daybreak and end fasting at sunset. It is thought that until then fasting was only broken for the duration of one meal at night. The month was defined as beginning with the new moon of the ninth month and ending with the new moon of *Shawwal,* the following month.

In this year the Prophet ﷺ married 'Aisha ﷺ, the young daughter of Abu Bakr ﷺ. She was very beautiful and mature though not yet a teenager. Her parents had been Muslim her whole life. The Prophet ﷺ had been a frequent visitor in their house and she had grown up loving and respecting him. Although he was fifty-three he appeared much younger. His hair and beard were still shining black and he was slim and handsome like a man of fewer years. Moving to his house made little change in 'Aisha's ﷺ everyday life. Her friends and playmates continued to visit her. Her mother and father lived nearby. The only change was that she got to spend more time in the company of the one she loved dearly, Muhammad ﷺ. She became the comfort and constant companion of the Prophet ﷺ until the day he passed away with his head in her lap. 'Aisha ﷺ was often present during the visits of Jibra'il ﷺ. She was able to hear his voice revealing new passages of the Quran. She had a wonderful memory and knew the Quran by heart. She also remembered all that the Prophet ﷺ said and all that he did. These were recorded and form part of the Hadith. She later taught both men and women who came to her to learn and have their questions answered.

The change that affected the Muslim community most was that Allah Almighty gave them permission to fight back against those who threatened them. They were encouraged to seek out their enemies, not just defend themselves. Sometimes it is necessary to use force, not in order to just get what you want, but to protect the Truth and establish Justice. They began to make life for the Meccans more difficult. They threatened the safety of the trade routes by raiding caravans returning laden with wealth. During the first year, at

least seven raids were conducted against Quraysh by the Muslims, some of which were led by the Prophet ﷺ himself.

On the first day of *Ramadan*, in the second year of the *Hijra*, Jibra'il ﷺ announced to the Prophet ﷺ the news of the arrival of a richly laden caravan under the leadership of Abu Sufyan ﷺ, who at that time was one of the chief unbelievers. Jibra'il ﷺ directed the Holy Prophet ﷺ to go out and fight. Victory would be his. The Prophet ﷺ chose to intercept the caravan at a place called Badr. He set out with an army of three hundred and ten men. Two were on horseback, seventy on camels and the rest on foot. The Prophet ﷺ led them mounted on Qaswa.

Abu Sufyan ﷺ had sent scouts ahead of the caravan to check the safety of the roads. Near the wells of Badr they saw in the distance some men on camels. In the waste left by the camels the scouts found date pits. Only camels from Medina ate dates, Abu Sufyan ﷺ reasoned. In this way he guessed that the Muslims of Medina were hunting his caravan. Abu Sufyan ﷺ took the caravan on a detour west to the sea to avoid being attacked. He sent a messenger to Mecca for reinforcements. The unbelievers of Mecca amassed a great army in order to protect the wealth of their city that was being transported in the caravan. A thousand armed and mounted men set out for Badr under the command of Abu Jahl.

The Muslims reached the wells of Badr first. Finding no trace of the caravan they set up camp. The Prophet ﷺ consulted his men. It was no longer a raid on a caravan that was being proposed in which the Muslims had surprise and numbers in their favor. They now faced a pitched battle with a much larger force. He wondered if the men of the *Ansar* would stand behind them. This was the first real test of their commitment to the Prophet ﷺ and Islam. When questioned, they rose as one and pledged their willingness to put their lives and property at the service of their Prophet ﷺ. Muhammad ﷺ was very moved at their loyalty and very pleased.

The Muslim army composed of three hundred and ten *Muhajirin* and *Ansar* together awaited the thousand-man army of Mecca. The next day the two armies came face to face. Abu Jahl saw the small number of the Muslims and he swelled with confidence and false pride. He made fun of the small force and shouted insults at them in his arrogance.

At first, three nobles from the Meccan army challenged the Muslims to single combat in the field separating the two armies. The Muslim warriors, 'Ali ❀, Hamza ❀ and 'Ubayda ❀ were victorious. Then the battle began in earnest. The Prophet ❀ stayed back and bent his head to the dusty ground in prayer, asking Allah to keep His promise and give victory to the small Muslim army. Jibra'il ❀ descended with a thousand angel warriors behind him, announcing the news of Allah's Peace and Victory. He brought a verse of Quran:

> *When you were praying to your Lord for help, He answered you: "I shall reinforce you with a thousand angels riding behind you."* (8:9)

The angels, mounted on horses of light, arranged themselves in rows, each one holding a spear in his hand. On their heads were black turbans, the long tails of which streamed out behind them when they rode. The Prophet ❀ scooped a handful of dust from the ground in front of him and threw it in the direction of the unbelievers. Allah caused a wind to arise that carried the dust into the eyes of the Meccans so that for a moment they could not see. The Muslims, supported by the angels, defeated the large Meccan army and killed many of its leaders.

Seventy-two of the Meccans were killed, among them Abu Jahl himself. Seventy-two were taken captive. The Prophet ﷺ kept the captives, even though the Meccans would have executed any Muslims had they captured them. He allowed their relatives to pay a ransom for their release in the hope that their hearts would open to Islam. Among the Muslims, only six *Muhajirin* and eight *Ansar* were martyred.

The Quraysh had taken 'Abbas ☙, the Prophet's ﷺ uncle, from his house by force and insisted he join their army. He and three of his nephews were captured on the battlefield. Afterwards 'Abbas ☙ was asked if he would pay the ransom for all four of them. He replied that he had nothing with which to pay. The Prophet ﷺ reminded him of the bag full of coins that he had secretly buried in his house. 'Abbas ☙ was startled. No one could possibly know of this money except he and his wife. He finally accepted Islam and took *shahada* from the Prophet ﷺ right then and there.

A poor man named Wahab ibn 'Umayr ☙ had one son who was captured at the battle of Badr. Wahab ☙ wanted to go to Medina to ransom him but he had no money. One of the chiefs of Quraysh, Safwan, promised Wahab ☙ that if he managed to kill Muhammad ﷺ while he was in Medina, Safwan would pay the ransom and raise Wahab's ☙ remaining children as his own in wealth and security. When Wahab ☙ approached the Prophet ﷺ in Medina, the Prophet ﷺ repeated this secret conversation with Safwan, word for word. Wahab ☙ accepted Islam and was sent back to Mecca by the Prophet ﷺ to secretly teach the new religion. Many people of Mecca came to Islam through Wahab ibn 'Umayr ☙.

The victorious Muslim army marched back to Medina. They were greeted by a joyous crowd. But there was also some sadness that awaited them. The Prophet's ﷺ dear daughter, Ruqayya ☙, the wife of 'Uthman ☙, had died while they were away.

Fatima ﷺ and 'Ali ﷜

After the victory at Badr the Muslims could not rest. Their enemies now knew they posed a significant threat. They began to make alliances in order to form a larger force with which to finally defeat the Muslims. The tribes of the Najd were gathering an army. The Prophet ﷺ took four hundred and fifty men and marched to Dhu Amarr where they were encamped. The enemy ran up into the hills when they saw the size of the Muslim army.

Earlier that day it had rained and the Prophet ﷺ was thoroughly drenched. After all danger seemed to be gone he removed his over clothes and hung them on bushes to dry. He lay down to sleep a little in the sun. The enemy, watching in the hills, saw him alone and unprotected. Their chief, named Du'thur ﷜, a fearless and merciless warrior, ran to where the Prophet ﷺ was lying and drew his sword. He cried, "Who will save you now from my might?"

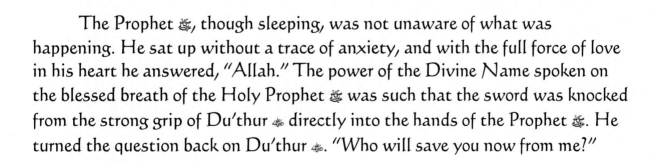

The Prophet ﷺ, though sleeping, was not unaware of what was happening. He sat up without a trace of anxiety, and with the full force of love in his heart he answered, "Allah." The power of the Divine Name spoken on the blessed breath of the Holy Prophet ﷺ was such that the sword was knocked from the strong grip of Du'thur ﷜ directly into the hands of the Prophet ﷺ. He turned the question back on Du'thur ﷜. "Who will save you now from me?"

At this moment Du'thur 🖈 came face to face with the power of prophethood and his hard heart melted in the light of Muhammad 🖈. He became Muslim while his men on the hillside tried to figure out what could possibly be happening. Du'thur 🖈 returned to them, his face shining, and a great many of them came to Islam through him. This story shows us that all things lie in the most powerful hands of Allah Almighty. In one instant the darkest and most vicious of men can be turned to the light and become merciful and good.

There arose another very significant threat to the new community. One of the tribes living in Medina, the Bani Qaynuqa, broke their peace treaty with the Prophet 🖈. They joined in an alliance with the enemy. When confronted with their treachery the Bani Qaynuqa were defiant. They locked themselves into their fortress and the Muslims laid siege at their gates. After some weeks the Bani Qaynuqa asked for mercy. In time of war mercy is rarely shown to a traitor, but the Prophet 🖈 allowed the Bani Qaynuqa to live and to leave Medina with all the wealth they could carry. The Muslims sadly watched them leave with their camels loaded with weapons and treasure to join their families in another oasis.

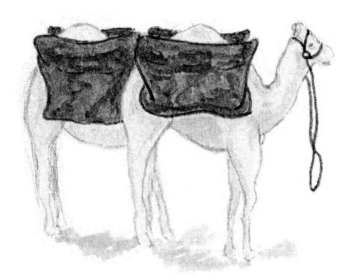

During this year there was also great happiness. The Prophet's 🖈 two daughters got married. Umm Kulthum 🖈 married 'Uthman 🖈. He had been married to her sister, Ruqayya 🖈, until her death the year before. Now 'Uthman 🖈 received the title of *Dhun Nurayn*, possessor of the two lights, husband to two daughters of the Prophet 🖈. 'Uthman 🖈 was a very handsome and gentle man who found it difficult to refuse anyone. He spent more time with his head to the ground in *sajda*, humble before his Lord, than any of the other close companions.

Also in this year the Prophet's ﷺ youngest daughter, Fatima ؓ, was married. She was the one of his children who was still a small child when Jibra'il ؑ began bringing the Quran. She grew up in Islam. People agreed that, of all his family, she most resembled her father. The rhythm of her speech, her walk and mannerisms were most like her father. She was called Fatima az-Zahra ؓ because she was like the delicate blossom of the orange tree, pure, beautiful and good. The Prophet ﷺ loved her dearly. When she entered the room he would stand up for her and seat her next to him by his right side. We stand out of respect for the members of the Prophet's ﷺ family who all descend from Fatima ؓ.

She was a young woman of eighteen or so years when they moved to Medina. There were many fine men who asked to marry her but the Prophet ﷺ waited for guidance from his Lord. Finally Jibra'il ؑ brought word to the Prophet ﷺ that Allah had already performed the marriage of Fatima ؓ to 'Ali ؓ in the Highest Heaven. The Prophet ﷺ should now do the same on Earth.

'Ali ؓ had not dared to ask for Fatima's ؓ hand before this. He felt shy to marry such a noble girl when he owned no house or property and had no money to his name. The Muslims at that time were forbidden to inherit anything from the unbelievers so that 'Ali ؓ had acquired nothing on the death of his father, Abu Talib. He was relieved and overjoyed that Allah had chosen him to marry Fatima ؓ.

'Ali ؓ was actually the cousin of the Prophet ﷺ, his uncle's son, but because of his youth he was raised in the Prophet's ﷺ household like his own son. Now he became also the son-in-law of the Prophet ﷺ. 'Ali

, though a child at the time, had been among the first to accept Islam. He stood up to his father and uncles in defending and supporting the Prophet ﷺ. He had grown into a fearless warrior whose sword with the twin points, named *Dhul Fikar*, became famous. He was also a scholar who memorized Quran and a master of the Arabic language. Beyond all this, he was a man of such a high spiritual station that the Prophet ﷺ called him his brother.

Fatima ؏ happily gave her consent and the wedding took place. It was a very simple ceremony. The Prophet ﷺ invited the companions to share some food and then he announced that he was giving Fatima ؏ to 'Ali ؏ in marriage, to love him and serve him provided that 'Ali ؏ also loved and served her. Then they joined the Prophet ﷺ in reciting *al-Fatiha*.

The Prophet ﷺ asked for a bowl of water. He drank some and sprinkled some drops with his right hand over Fatima's ؏ chest. He sprinkled some more water over the back and shoulders of 'Ali ؏ and he prayed to Allah to give them happiness and abundance.

Then Jibra'il ؏ appeared and asked Fatima ؏ what she desired from Allah Almighty for her dowry. She thanked Allah with all her heart for all that He had already given her. Then she shyly asked that on the Day of Judgment she be allowed to ask forgiveness for the weak nation of Muslims. Allah granted her only wish and made her the helper of her father who was sent as a mercy to the worlds.

Jibra'il ؏ handed her a paper on which this promise was written. He and the Prophet ﷺ signed the marriage contract and these two papers were rolled up and placed inside a sealed glass. Years later, when she lay dying, Fatima ؏ asked 'Ali ؏ to bring her that glass. She clasped it tightly in her hands so as to be ready to present it to Allah Almighty when the time came.

Fatima az-Zahra ؏ entered married life with six material gifts. She had a woven mat for a bed, a leather pillow stuffed with palm fiber, a goatskin to hold drinking water, a basket and two bowls. Her intention

was to set an example she thought all women, whatever their worldly circumstances, could follow. She received no expensive gifts. She celebrated with no elaborate feast. The gifts she brought to her marriage were her purity, her generosity and her human kindness. The gift she received for her marriage was Allah's forgiveness for all of us.

21

The Battle of Uhud

The Quraysh were humiliated by their defeat at Badr the year before. Many of their leaders had been killed. The wives and mothers of the dead called those who returned cowards. These accusations fueled their anger and made them insistent upon another battle. The wife of Abu Sufyan ﷺ, Hind, offered a fortune to one man if he would kill the Prophet's ﷺ uncle, Hamza ﷺ, who had killed her father at Badr. The Quraysh were thirsting for revenge. They assembled an enormous army of three thousand men. They were well outfitted, each wore two suits of chain mail and many were on horseback.

'Abbas ﷺ, the Prophet's ﷺ uncle, who had kept his Islam secret, now sent a letter to warn the Prophet ﷺ that the Quraysh were organizing a new military campaign. The Prophet ﷺ called his companions to discuss what action should be taken. He thought they should remain within the safety of the walls of the city, but the young Muslims were confident after the success of Badr and anxious to test their fighting skills. They urged the Prophet ﷺ to go out to engage the enemy in a standing battle. The Prophet ﷺ went home, put on his chain mail, wound his turban around his helmet, girded his sword and slung his shield over his shoulder. He mounted his camel, Qaswa, and prepared to lead the army. By then the young warriors felt ashamed that they had gone contrary to the Prophet's ﷺ advice. The

Prophet ﷺ, however, said that once the sword of a prophet is put on it cannot be removed until battle is waged. At this three hundred of the thousand-man army

deserted and hid in their houses. The Muslim army, now just seven hundred strong, moved onto the plain at the foot of the mountain called Uhud.

There they would meet the Meccan army of three thousand well-equipped soldiers. This army was commanded by men of courage and military genius. Later in fact, when belief had entered their hearts, they would lead the Muslim armies to victory all over the world. They made a formidable enemy.

The Prophet ﷺ carefully arranged his soldiers. He chose fifty of his best archers and stationed them on a rise to the left of the main force. He instructed them that they were not to leave their position until he personally gave the order to do so, regardless of what happened, even if they saw the Muslims gain victory or fall back in defeat. Even if they should see all the Muslims being slaughtered they were not to leave in order to try to help.

The Meccan army marched to war to the beat of drums and tambourines. The women sang crude songs challenging their men to do battle and win the

rewards of their wives. The Muslim army followed their Prophet ﷺ, making *dhikr*. They called, "Allah, Allah," until the earth itself vibrated with their chant. The Prophet ﷺ drew out one of his engraved swords and asked who would take it and do right by it. Abu Dujanah ؓ asked him, "What is its right?" The Prophet ﷺ answered,

"To fight until it is bent in Allah's Way." Then Abu Dujanah ؓ offered to take the sword.

The two sides engaged in battle and fought with fury. But the Muslims gained the upper hand because even though they were few in numbers they completely believed in the cause for which they were fighting and were unafraid of death. Abu Dujanah ؓ fought like ten men. He cut a path through the entire enemy until he reached the women beating their drums and singing rude songs at the very rear of the army. He raised his sword above the head of Hind and then reconsidered. He did not want to dishonor the

blade of the Prophet ﷺ by taking the life of a woman. He turned and fought his way back to the Muslim side. On the way he was mortally wounded. He fell and turned his head towards the Prophet ﷺ and prayed to die while gazing at his blessed face. The Prophet ﷺ heard his wish and ordered him to be brought near. He died by the side of his beloved Prophet ﷺ.

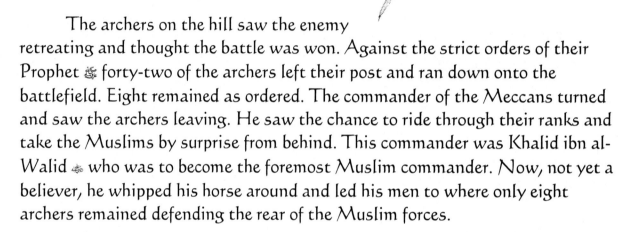

'Ali ﷺ fought until there was not a family of Mecca who was untouched by his sword. Hamza ﷺ stuck a peacock plume in his turban so that all who wanted could find him easily. Hamza ﷺ and 'Ali ﷺ were by themselves equivalent to a whole army. The Meccans began to pull back.

The archers on the hill saw the enemy retreating and thought the battle was won. Against the strict orders of their Prophet ﷺ forty-two of the archers left their post and ran down onto the battlefield. Eight remained as ordered. The commander of the Meccans turned and saw the archers leaving. He saw the chance to ride through their ranks and take the Muslims by surprise from behind. This commander was Khalid ibn al-Walid ﷺ who was to become the foremost Muslim commander. Now, not yet a believer, he whipped his horse around and led his men to where only eight archers remained defending the rear of the Muslim forces.

The archers fought valiantly but were no match for the large numbers of Quraysh. They all fell, killed as martyrs. The rest of the Meccan army saw this happen and turned back to renew the battle. The tide had turned. The Muslims were now on the defensive. The man Hind had paid to kill Hamza ﷺ saw his chance and accomplished his terrible deed. Then someone called out that they had seen the Prophet ﷺ himself fall. On hearing this, the Muslim army lost heart and fell into disarray. Even the mighty 'Umar ﷺ dropped his sword to his side and did not have the heart to lift it.

But the Prophet ﷺ had not been struck down. He was just in a low part of the field where he could not be seen. In all the confusion only twelve companions were with him to protect him. Among them was Nusayba ﷺ, one of

the two women who had pledged herself to the Prophet ﷺ at 'Aqaba. She threw herself at the enemy, swinging her sword at anyone who came near.

Then Ka'b ibn Malik ؓ caught sight of the Prophet ﷺ. All that was visible through the slit in his helmet and the grime of the battlefield were his eyes. But those eyes were like no others and whoever saw them would know them anywhere. He called out in joy so loudly that all the Muslims heard, "The Prophet ﷺ lives. He is here." The Muslims came running from all over the field to defend their Prophet ﷺ, but of course the enemy also heard his cry and came running as well.

The blessed Prophet ﷺ then came under fierce attack. The Muslims laid themselves over the Prophet ﷺ in order to shield him with their bodies. Many of them were killed. One of the companions had forty arrows sticking out of him. Another lady warrior, Umm Ummara ؓ, joined in protecting the Prophet ﷺ and

was struck a terrible blow. Sa'd ibn Abi Waqqas ؓ stood firm and shot arrows handed to him directly by the Prophet ﷺ. Each one found its mark. The Prophet ﷺ blessed him and asked that his prayers be accepted. Later in life when he had become sick and blind, his companions asked Sa'd ؓ why he did not pray to be healed. He answered that the Will of his Lord was more precious to him than all the health in the world. The gift of getting whatever you want is only given to those who want nothing other than what Allah has already given.

In the heat of battle the Prophet ﷺ was wounded. He was hit in the mouth and broke a tooth and then hit on the side of the head so hard that two links of his chain mail became imbedded in his cheek. Abu 'Ubayda ؓ removed these links with his lips and teeth for fear that his hands were too large and rough and might further injure the blessed Prophet ﷺ. In the process, Abu 'Ubayda ؓ himself broke two teeth but felt no pain because of the great joy at being so close to the face of the Prophet ﷺ.

During the entire battle the Prophet ﷺ prayed to Allah to protect the Muslims, but never once did he ask Allah to destroy the enemy. He only asked Allah to forgive them, to change their hearts and bring them to Islam.

The Meccans had nearly achieved their goals, to destroy the Prophet ﷺ and the Muslims. But the Muslim army had recovered. They protected themselves and their Prophet ﷺ at great cost. The Meccans, feeling satisfied and thinking they had accomplished their aims, withdrew from the field. Abu Sufyan ؓ called out as he was leaving, "Victory goes in turns. You won at Badr. We have won today. We are now equal." The Prophet ﷺ had 'Umar ؓ call back, "We are not equal. Our dead are in Paradise. Your dead are in the fire."

The Muslims looked out over the field of battle. Quraysh had lost only thirty men out of three thousand. The Muslims had lost fully seventy out of seven hundred, each one of greater value than a crowd of other men. The Muslims began to collect their dead and tend to their wounded. The Prophet ﷺ gazed at each martyr individually. His eyes filled with tears. When he saw his uncle, Hamza ؓ, he was unable to bear the sorrow until Allah Almighty showed him Hamza's ؓ high station in the Divine Presence.

The dead were quickly buried. Those who loved each other were put together in one grave, and the Prophet ﷺ prayed the funeral prayer over each one. Allah revealed a verse of Quran:

> Count not those who were slain in Allah's Way as dead,
> but rather living with their Lord. (3:164)

Uhud was a hard lesson for the Muslims. Victory cannot be taken for granted. Allah will continue to test the believers with difficulties. Those whose hearts are true and remain patient will become stronger for it. The Muslims had

gone against the wishes of their Prophet ﷺ twice, once in leaving the walls of Medina to do battle and once when the archers deserted their post. In addition most of the enemy were destined one day to become believers. They were brought a little closer to this day by seeing the moral strength and dedication of the Muslims, and the degree to which they loved Muhammad ﷺ. The battle of Uhud was a severe test for the Muslims but sometimes there is more to be learned from failure than from success.

The Battle of the Trench

After Uhud the Quraysh continued to avenge themselves on the Muslims. A Muslim from any tribe other than Quraysh was considered fair game. He could be killed without mercy. An outlying tribe asked the Prophet ﷺ to send them some young men to instruct them in Islam. These young Muslims were ambushed and killed. Only two survived and were sold to Quraysh who tortured and then killed them in revenge for two of their own who had died in battle. No Muslim families were given the chance to ransom these loved ones. The struggle between the Muslims and the unbelievers intensified and became more ugly and treacherous.

As Islam spread so did the opposition to it. The Quraysh began to call on their friends and allies from wherever they could find them. They even approached the many Jewish tribes living in Medina. The Bani Nadir became the second tribe of Medina to go over to the enemy. They broke their treaty of peace and assistance with the Prophet ﷺ by providing help and encouragement to the Quraysh. The Bani Nadir, like the Bani Qaynuqa before them, were banished from the city of Medina.

The Muslims again sadly watched as their powerful and wealthy former allies loaded their wives and children, gold and jewels on camels and paraded defiantly out of the city. They went to join their relatives, the Bani Qaynuqa, in the not too distant oasis of Khaybar. This time, however, the Prophet ﷺ made them leave their weapons

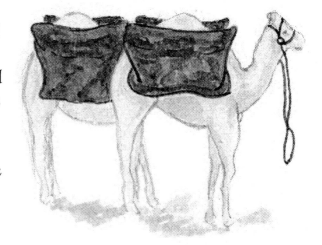

and armor behind them because the Muslims were in dire need of them. The Prophet ﷺ had been forced to turn poor, young soldiers away because there were no weapons for them to use.

The Quraysh assembled an enormous fighting force of thirty thousand men committed to the destruction of Islam. They marched on Medina with the intention of leveling it and everyone in it. The tribes of Khaybar began to pressure the Bani Qurayza tribe who still lived in Medina, to break

their peace treaty with the Prophet ﷺ and join the enemy alliance. The Bani Qurayza were of real importance to the Muslims. Medina is situated on an open plain. Three sides of the city were protected from attack by high buildings built close together so as to form a wall. Two of these sides belonged to Muslims but the third side belonged to the Bani Qurayza. The Muslims were depending on the Bani Qurayza to defend their side of the city.

The fourth side of Medina was an open field and the Prophet ﷺ decided to station his army there for he assumed the Quraysh would attack at this, their weakest point. The Prophet ﷺ consulted the Muslims as he always did before coming to a decision. At this meeting a man rose to give his advice. His name was Salman ﷺ. He had been born in Persia to a noble family of fire worshippers. As a young man he had become Christian and run away from his home to attach himself in service to a devout Christian monk. While living with him Salman ﷺ learned that a prophet was expected in the near future to appear in Arabia. It became the desire of his heart to meet and serve this prophet. When the Christian monk died, Salman ﷺ determined to go to Arabia in order to be nearby when this prophet appeared.

On his journey he was captured by slave traders and sold into slavery. By Allah's Divine Plan he was bought by a man of Medina. When the Prophet ﷺ arrived in Medina, Salman ◉ was watching from the top of a date palm. A few days later he got permission from his master to visit the Prophet ﷺ. In Muhammad ﷺ Salman ◉ recognized all the signs of prophecy and he took his hand and declared his Islam.

Many of the first and most distinguished of the Muslims came from among those who were called slaves. Slavery was a terrible reality in Arabia at that time and around the world. Sometimes people were taken as captives in war and sold as slaves. Sometimes children were kidnapped from their families and bought and sold like property. They came from all backgrounds and nationalities and races.

Zayd ◉ was an Arab taken hostage by an enemy Arab tribe. He was sold into slavery and bought by Khadija ◉ as a gift for Muhammad ﷺ. The Prophet ﷺ treated his slave with great kindness and raised him like a son. After several years Zayd's ◉ father learned of his whereabouts and traveled to Mecca in an attempt to gain the freedom of his son. The Prophet ﷺ offered Zayd ◉ a choice. He could return with his father to his native land or he could stay where he was as part of the Prophet's ﷺ family. In either case he would be free. Zayd ◉ hugged his father and explained that he could not leave Muhammad ﷺ whom he loved more than his own life. His father felt content that his son had found a home better than the one into which he had been born. He returned home alone. Zayd ◉ continued to grow to manhood as a member of the Prophet's ﷺ household. All his life the Prophet ﷺ showed his great love for Zayd ◉. The Companions loved him also because their Prophet ﷺ did. Zayd ◉ was put as a commander over them and these noble warriors humbly obeyed even though he had once been a slave, because his authority came from Allah.

Bilal ◉ also had been a slave. He was from Abyssinia in Africa and had been sold to a member of Quraysh. His master was hard and cruel. After Bilal

⚜ accepted Islam his master tortured him without mercy. But nothing could make Bilal ⚜ turn back on his Islam, certainly not the threat of death. Abu Bakr ⚜ managed, after many attempts, to offer enough money to free Bilal ⚜ from his

oppressor. Bilal ⚜ then devoted himself to the Prophet ﷺ and Islam. Because of his beautiful strong voice he was made *muadhdhin* of the Muslims. Because of his true heart the Prophet ﷺ heard his footsteps ahead of him in the Highest Heaven.

Slavery no longer exists but there are still people who think that because they are rich or powerful or come from a noble family they are better than others who are poor or weak. The Prophet ﷺ showed us by his example that the difference between people lies only in the quality of their hearts, not in the quality of their worldly circumstances. Allah said in the Quran:
Surely the best among you in the sight of Allah is the most pious among you. Allah is all knowing and aware of all things. (49:13)

At this time in Medina, Salman ⚜, the Persian slave, spoke up in the war council of the Muslims. In Persia he had seen them dig a deep ditch, rather than build a wall, around their cities in order to protect them. The Prophet ﷺ liked this idea and decided it was possible for them to do. For two weeks the Muslim army, and anyone else who was able, dug a trench on the northern edge of Medina. Women and children helped carry away the rocks and dirt. The Prophet ﷺ himself took off his shirt and labored in the dust and dirt alongside the others. While they worked he led the Muslims in chants to remind them of the Almighty Lord for Whose Pleasure they struggled.

Sometimes they came across a boulder they were unable to break or remove. Then they called the Prophet ﷺ. He hit it with his pick while he breathed the words, "*Bismillah.*" The boulder would crumble to pieces. One time they saw sparks fly when he struck

a boulder. The first spark lit up the sky until they could see the red roofs of Damascus. The second spark lit the sky until they could see the city of San'a in the Yeman. The third spark lit up the sky until the capital of Persia came within sight.

The Muslims were exhausted and dust-covered, but also exhilarated. The Prophet ﷺ loved to remember those days of the Trench when all the believers worked together in perfect unity for the love of Allah and His Prophet ﷺ. They might have been hungry and dirty but the light that shone on their faces made them beautiful.

The trench was just finished when the enemy army of thirty thousand men rode up, singing and drumming in their arrogance. They stopped short at

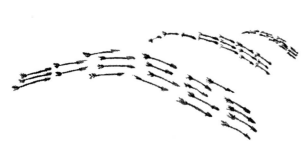

the edge of the trench. They had never seen anything like this before and they did not know how to proceed. Their horses could not jump the trench. If they slid down the side into it they would become an easy target for the Muslim archers standing above them on the other side. They set up camp on the far side and kept shooting a rain of arrows across the trench. At one point their most famous warrior jumped into the trench and challenged any of the Muslims to fight him. 'Ali ﷺ responded to the challenge and put an end to him. The enemy army watched in disbelief. No one else followed. They watched and waited.

The Muslim army waited also. They took turns sleeping and keeping watch. They were already tired from digging the trench. They continued to get little rest because they expected the enemy to attack at any time. For the first time ever the Muslims had to let four prayers go by without praying because of the constant threat and the rain of arrows. They remembered it as a time of great fear and hardship.

Finally after twenty days, in answer to His Prophet's ﷺ prayer, Allah sent invisible help in the form of a cold, fierce wind. It blew down the enemy's

tents and scattered their stores of grain. It blew out their fires so that they were cold and had nothing to eat. Their animals sickened and died. Without a strong belief in the cause for which they were fighting, the weak among them began to sneak away and return home.

The biggest threat, however, lay behind the Muslims. The Bani Qurayzah were negotiating with Quraysh to turn traitor and attack the Muslims from behind. A new Muslim named Nu'aym ﷺ concocted a clever scheme. He was a friend to both the Bani Qurayzah and the Quraysh. Neither of them knew that he had accepted Islam. He went to the Bani Qurayzah and told them that the Quraysh were planning to betray them. Once they attacked the Muslims the Quraysh would not join them in support. Then Nu'aym ﷺ visited Abu Sufyan ﷺ on the Quraysh side and convinced him that the Bani Qurayzah were planning to betray them. He managed, with Allah's help, to convince the two that each was planning to betray the other. Their alliance dissolved.

After twenty torturous days of waiting and twenty cold, wet, and miserable nights, Abu Sufyan ﷺ announced he had had enough. He mounted his horse and left. With their commander suddenly gone, the army, little by little, broke up. Ragged and discouraged they crept back to their homes. The Muslims woke up in the morning and the enemy had disappeared. Only five Muslims had lost their lives.

The Bani Qurayza were judged for their treachery according to their own law.

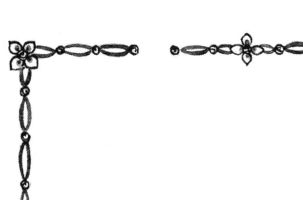

23

The Treaty of Hudaybiyah

The Prophet ﷺ fasted *Ramadan* in Medina and then announced to the Muslims that they were to prepare themselves for the lesser pilgrimage. It had been six years since any of them had prayed at the Ka'aba. It was time to return to Mecca as peaceful pilgrims.

The Prophet ﷺ mounted Qaswa, his trusty camel, who had carried him into Medina, and set out with fifteen hundred pilgrims for Mecca. When they reached the well of Hudaybiyah, on the outskirts of Mecca, Qaswa stopped and knelt down. They pulled her and shouted at her but she would not budge. The companions suggested that maybe she was tired. But the Prophet ﷺ knew that was not her character. He told them she was being guided, just as the elephant, Mahmud, had been guided. So the Muslims made camp at Hudaybiyah, by Allah's order conveyed to them through Qaswa.

The men and animals were tired and thirsty from their long journey. They tried to draw water from the well only to find there was none. The Prophet ﷺ instructed one of his companions to bring him the one bucket of muddy water they had been able to collect. With this he made his *wudu'.* Then he spit some of the water from his blessed mouth back into the bucket. Handing his companion one of his arrows, he told him to climb down into the well and 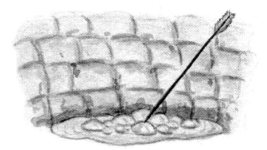 stir the contents of the bucket into the mud at the bottom. As soon as the arrow touched the mud, clean water began to bubble up from the ground. It gushed so quickly that the man had to jump out before he was soaked.

Now the Prophet ﷺ called for 'Umar ﷺ. He planned to send him to Mecca to tell Quraysh that the Muslims were coming in peace with the single intention of visiting the Holy House. 'Umar ﷺ, however, expressed his concern. He knew he was a man quick to anger. He felt he might not be able to restrain himself when faced with the insulting attitude of the Quraysh towards the Prophet ﷺ. He suggested that the Prophet ﷺ send 'Uthman ﷺ instead, as he was mild mannered and well liked. He would be better able to communicate the Prophet's ﷺ message of peace. 'Uthman ﷺ was sent. He found the Quraysh absolutely unwilling to allow the Muslims to enter their city. They offered to let him visit the Ka'aba but 'Uthman ﷺ refused. If the Prophet ﷺ was not allowed to pray there, then he would not pray there either.

The Quraysh sent a representative to the Prophet ﷺ. His name was 'Urwa and his intention was to prevent bloodshed. He explained how hostile the Quraysh were and how large an army of friends and allies they could assemble if the Muslims persisted in approaching Mecca. He suggested the Muslims go home and forget about making the pilgrimage. The companions could hardly restrain themselves when they heard the unintentionally rude

manner in which he addressed the Prophet ﷺ. Even 'Urwa's own nephew, who was a Muslim, threatened him if he dared continue to speak. 'Urwa returned to Mecca completely amazed. He told the Quraysh that in all his experience in the courts of kings and sultans, from Persia to Byzantium, he had never seen anyone treated with the love and respect with which he saw the Muslims treat Muhammad ﷺ. When the Prophet ﷺ spoke there was absolute silence. When he washed they caught the falling water to use themselves. If a hair on his head or beard became loose they saved it and treasured it. There was no way, he advised, that the Muslims would ever give up their struggle. They would follow Muhammad ﷺ faithfully to the end. It was time to talk and not to fight.

Members of an allied tribe who were present at this meeting heard 'Urwa and became curious to see this man who commanded such total loyalty. They went to visit the Muslims at Hudaybiyah. They saw men and women dressed for pilgrimage, without weapons and with their faces full of light. They returned to Quraysh and expressed their deep disapproval. Even if the Arabs had forgotten the worship of Allah, they had remembered that the Ka'aba was a sacred place. The Quraysh were considered to have the privilege of guarding the Ka'aba. They did not own it. Their position was dependent on their keeping it open and safe for all who wanted to visit. It was not their right to turn away any sincere pilgrim. If the Quraysh insisted on denying the Muslims permission to visit the Ka'aba, then their allies would desert them and align themselves with the Muslims.

The Quraysh now faced a real dilemma. They sent another of their leaders, named Suhayl, to negotiate with the Prophet ﷺ. Suhayl asked the Muslims to return home without making the pilgrimage. If they were allowed to enter Mecca it would appear as if the Quraysh were weak and defeated. Next year, he promised, the Muslims could return. The Quraysh would leave the city and for three days the Prophet ﷺ and his companions could have the Ka'aba to themselves. The Prophet ﷺ accepted this compromise and directed 'Ali ﷺ to write the agreement down on paper.

When 'Ali ﷺ wrote "Muhammad *Rasulullah* ﷺ," the Prophet of Allah, Suhayl objected. He said, quite frankly, that if he accepted that Muhammad ﷺ was truly "*rasulullah,*" then there would be no need for these negotiations. The Prophet ﷺ, in his gentleness, instructed 'Ali ﷺ to cross out where he had written "*rasulullah.*" Ali ﷺ had never before disobeyed the Prophet ﷺ. Until that time whatever he had been asked to do he did without hesitation, but to cross out "*rasulullah*" he just could not do. It was the Truth and could not be erased. The Prophet ﷺ had to cross it out with his own hand and write the name by which he was known in Mecca, Muhammad, son of Abdullah ﷺ. The Muslims were growing more and more upset.

Suhayl and the Prophet ﷺ agreed to put an end to the bloodshed. There would be no more killing. The Prophet ﷺ agreed to end the pilgrimage that year at Hudaybiyah and to return the following year. Then Mecca would be turned over to the Muslims for three days.

Suhayl, who himself had a son who had accepted Islam and who he kept locked in chains in the house, insisted that the Prophet ﷺ agree to more terms. The Muslims listened in fury as Suhayl proposed that any man of Quraysh who fled to Medina without the permission of his family would have to be returned to Mecca. Any Muslim, however, who fled to Mecca did not have to be returned. The companions immediately started to grumble at such unfair terms. But the Prophet ﷺ, to their disbelief, accepted them. No Muslim, after all, ever tried to return to Mecca.

This agreement was just being finished and signed when Abu Jandal ﷺ, Suhayl's Muslim son, staggered into the meeting, his chains dragging behind him. He fell at the feet of the Prophet ﷺ crying tears of joy. He had finally

managed to escape his cruel father and join the Beloved Prophet ﷺ. Suhayl demanded the immediate return of his son, or the peace treaty would be considered broken. To the horror and anguish of the Muslims, Abu Jandal ﷺ was handed sobbing to his father, but not before the Prophet ﷺ gave him comfort. Looking him in the eyes he told him to keep courage, that Allah was witness to his grief and would make a way for him.

The companions were severely tested with the Treaty of Hudaybiyah. They could not see what the Prophet ﷺ saw. They could not understand what the Prophet ﷺ understood. To the companions it looked like what was right and just was giving way to what was wrong and cruel. It felt like defeat. It was, in fact, the first sign of the coming total victory of Islam.

The companions did not understand, and they were disheartened and depressed. The Prophet ﷺ called them to him in the shade of a large acacia tree and asked them to renew their oath of loyalty, or *ba'yat*, to him. One by one

they took his hand and pledged themselves to Islam and to their Prophet ﷺ. They might be hurt and confused but their loyalty was never shaken. A verse of Quran was revealed:

> *Allah was well pleased with the believers when they were swearing loyalty to you under the tree and He knew what was in their hearts, so He sent down His Peace upon them and rewarded them with a coming victory and many benefits; and Allah is ever All Mighty, All Wise.* (48:18)

The Muslims returned to Medina not knowing that a victory had been won. Little by little they came to understand. They were now at peace. They did not have to spend all their time and energy fighting for their lives. Their friends and relatives could visit them in Medina in safety and see for themselves the condition of the Muslims. The Muslims in turn could travel and speak about Islam openly and freely. Until this time most of the people of Arabia had only heard vicious lies about the new religion and its Prophet ﷺ. Now they were able to see with their own eyes the light on the faces of the believers and to hear Quran recited. They realized that they were only being called to the Truth. In the next year more people entered Islam than in all the previous years. Now all the companions could see that what had looked like a defeat had been in fact a great victory.

During this year another young man of Quraysh, who was being abused by his family because of his Islam, escaped and made his way to Medina. His name was 'Utba bin Asid ﷺ. The Prophet ﷺ had to turn him over to the men his family had sent to retrieve him. On their way back to Mecca he escaped from his captors and found safety in the mountains along the shore. Other young Muslims escaped from Mecca to join him, including Abu Jandal ﷺ. They began raiding the caravans of Quraysh that passed that way. After a while the Quraysh begged the Prophet ﷺ to take these young men into his control in Medina so that the roads would be safe again. In this way the most distasteful part of the Treaty of Hudaybiyah was dissolved without breaking the peace.

The Letters

When the Muslims were digging the trench they had come across one large boulder that they had been unable to lift or break. They had called the Prophet ﷺ who, with his pickaxe and his "*Bismillah,*" had shattered the boulder into three pieces. With each blow a spark had lit up the sky. With the first spark they could see as far as Damascus in Syria. With the second spark the Yemen became visible. With the third spark they saw the capital city of Persia. This was a sign for the Prophet ﷺ, Salman ؓ and the others who witnessed it. Islam was destined to spread beyond the borders of Arabia. It was a religion for the whole world brought by a Prophet ﷺ for the whole world. At this time a new verse of Quran was revealed:

> *And We have not sent you except as a mercy to all the worlds.*
> (21:107)

The Prophet ﷺ, in the relative peace that followed Hudaybiyah, set about informing the great kings and sultans of the world about Allah, His Prophets and His Quran. He dictated letters inviting the kings and their subjects to accept Islam. One letter the Prophet ﷺ sent to Heraclius, the Christian Emperor of Byzantium whose capital was at Constantinople, now Istanbul. He had just fought and won a war against Persian forces and was in Jerusalem celebrating. The letter reached him there. On reading it he called for his servants to search the marketplace and bring him any Arabs they could find from the area of Mecca. He wanted to question them about the author of the letter.

It so happened that Abu Sufyan ☙, one of the leaders of Quraysh, was doing business in Jerusalem at the time. He and his companions went to meet with the Emperor. Heraclius was seated on his throne in his royal pavilion, his crown on his head, his advisors and Christian bishops around him. He began questioning the Arabs. He wanted to know who among them was related most closely to this man, Muhammad ☙, who called himself the Prophet of God. Abu Sufyan ☙ answered that he was, so Heraclius addressed all his questions to him.

Abu Sufyan ☙ was still a declared enemy of the Prophet ☙, but standing before the Emperor with his companions as witnesses he was afraid to do anything but tell the complete truth. He told the Emperor that Muhammad ☙ came from one of the most noble families of Arabia, and that no one among his relatives had ever been known to claim to be a prophet before. He said that mostly the poor followed him, and that every day their numbers increased and none of them ever left his following. Then Heraclius asked Abu Sufyan ☙ if Muhammad ☙ had ever been known to tell a lie. Abu Sufyan ☙ could only answer that in all honesty he had never heard him say anything untrue. The Emperor wanted to know what exactly Muhammad ☙ was teaching. Abu Sufyan ☙ said that he was trying to tell them about the One God Who alone is worthy of worship, Who created everything and loves and cares for all His creation. Abu Sufyan ☙ then added that Muhammad ☙ hated all idols and criticized other religions, including the Christian religion of Heraclius because he said it had been changed and corrupted.

The Emperor listened to all this closely and then announced that he had no doubt that Muhammad ☙ was in fact the Messenger of God. He wished with all his heart that he were able to travel to Medina to visit him. He ordered the letter to be read out loud through the streets of his kingdom. His officials and his priests, however, were not so accepting. If the Emperor became Muslim they would lose their jobs and power. They let him know that should he follow his heart and become Muslim they would oppose him and destroy his kingship.

Heraclius became fearful. Although he felt the light of faith rising in his heart, his love for his own kingly wealth and position threw a thick veil over it and in the end covered the light entirely.

The Prophet ﷺ sent a second letter to Khosru, the king of Persia, who considered himself like a god. When he saw the beginning of the letter, which read, "From Muhammad, Prophet of Allah, to Parviz, Shah of Persia," his anger flared. How dare this unknown man from Arabia put his own name on the same line as the ruler of Persia? He saw nothing more and felt nothing more. In his anger he tore the Prophet's ﷺ  letter into little pieces. Later the Prophet ﷺ would say that it was as if Khosru had torn his own kingdom to pieces. After his death the kingdom of Persia did break apart into many small kingdoms, all of which eventually came to Islam.

At this time Yemen was under the rule of the Persian Empire. Khosru sent a letter to the king of Yemen, Badhan ؓ, ordering him to send two men to Medina to escort the Prophet ﷺ to Persia to apologize to the king. The Holy Prophet ﷺ greeted the two men with hospitality and told them he would talk with them in the morning. That night Allah informed the Prophet ﷺ that Parviz, the king, had been killed by his own son, Shirawayh. The next morning the Prophet ﷺ told this to the envoys from Yemen and asked them to return to Badhan ؓ and invite him to Islam. They returned to King Badhan ؓ, who informed them that in fact, as Muhammad ﷺ had said, Parviz had died. Badhan ؓ himself immediately accepted Islam and became the first Muslim governor of Yemen.

A third letter was sent to the Negus of Abyssinia. He was a Christian king who had already given refuge and help to the Muslims. Some of the Muslims were still living in his country. The Negus summoned one of these Muslims, Ja'far ibn Abi Talib ؓ, the brother of 'Ali ؓ. He asked him to stand as witness that he, the Negus of Abyssinia, accepted Islam and the prophecy of Muhammad ﷺ. Then he sent his own son with sixty men to pledge their allegiance to the Prophet ﷺ in person. By Allah's will, however, the ship that carried them sank in the Red Sea and they all drowned.

A fourth letter was taken by one of the companions to the Muqawqis, leader of the Coptic Christians of Egypt. He responded by sending valuable

gifts back to the Prophet ﷺ. He sent two pure and beautiful slave girls, Maryam ؆ and Sirin ؆, whom he said occupied a place of honor among them. He also sent a fine robe and a white mule which became the Prophet's ﷺ mount and which he named *Duldul.* But in the letter that accompanied the gifts it was unclear whether the Muqawqis had actually accepted Islam or not.

By the time the Coptic sisters reached Medina, Islam had entered their hearts. They declared their belief when they reached the Holy Prophet ﷺ. One of them, Maryam ؆, the Prophet ﷺ married, and the other he married to one of his close companions. Both became free.

Other letters were also sent to the leaders of the most powerful tribes inviting them all to Islam. Most of these chieftains, like most of the kings, chose their pride and position in this world over Truth and joy in the hereafter, and did not become Muslim.

25

The Battle of Khaybar

When the Prophet ﷺ first arrived in Medina he had hoped the tribes living there who followed the Old Testament would easily recognize his message and become Muslim. He approached them with respect and offered them a warm welcome. He was disappointed to find them as strong in their opposition to him as his own family of Quraysh in Mecca. These had been the only tribes of believers in Arabia and had become proud of this fact and thought it was their right. For centuries they had been living among the idol-worshipping Arabs who had never shown any interest in learning about the One God. So, while they were expecting a prophet to come, they thought he would be sent to lead them to victory over the unbelievers. When that Prophet ﷺ finally came, by Allah's command, from a tribe of idol worshippers, most of the the believers in earlier holy books could not accept him. Some of their scholars even recognized the signs of Prophethood in Muhammad ﷺ but were prevented from accepting him because of their false expectations and their pride. They were really no different from the Arab tribes, including Quraysh, or from the kings and rulers to whom letters were sent. They could not accept that God would send a prophet other than from among themselves. Pride and arrogance can be an insurmountable barrier to faith and we must all be careful to keep our hearts humble and accepting. As we have seen earlier, Allah can honor whom He wishes and humiliate whom He wishes.

Of course, not all of the Jews rejected Islam. Many individuals felt their hearts fill with love and belief. They left their families and homes to take the hand of the Prophet ﷺ. Some of them fought at Badr and Uhud. One tribal leader accepted Islam and tried, without success, to bring his entire family with him.

After the Muslims made the Peace Treaty of Hudaybiyah with the tribes of Quraysh, there still remained one major threat. This came from the tribes living at Khaybar, an oasis three days journey north of Medina. It was with the tribes of Khaybar that the Bani Nadhir and Bani Qaynuqa had taken refuge. They were steadfast in their opposition to the Muslims. Because they were very wealthy, they helped organize and pay for the attack on Medina that resulted in the battle of the Trench. After its failure they offered money and arms to anyone who would fight the Muslims. The Prophet ﷺ got word that they were assembling a large army and planned to attack Medina again.

In the seventh year of the *Hijra* at the beginning of the month of *Muharram,* one thousand four hundred Muslims marched under the command of their Prophet ﷺ to Khaybar. Their aim was to prevent an army from organizing and marching on Medina. 'Ali ؓ carried the Muslim banner, which was made from the headscarf of 'Aisha ؓ. The Prophet's ﷺ wives came with them to tend to the wounded and bring water and arrows to the fighters.

The Muslims reached Khaybar at night. The Prophet ﷺ told the army to rest. In the morning they would approach the enemy and see if they were really intent upon fighting. The Prophet ﷺ hoped they would see the Muslim forces and decide to make peace. But in the morning it became clear that the army of Khaybar had chosen war. There were twenty thousand fighting men behind the walls of Khaybar. They were completely confident of victory.

The fortresses of Khaybar fell to the Muslim army one after another, until only one was left. This was the largest fort whose walls were impossible to climb or to shatter. The first day Abu Bakr ؓ led the troops in the assault but he could not break through. The next day the Prophet ﷺ sent 'Umar ؓ to lead the troops, but he also could not win a victory. That night the Prophet ﷺ announced that in the morning he would send a commander loved by Allah and His Prophet ﷺ who would at last secure a victory for the Muslims.

All night the Muslims wondered who that champion would be. In the morning they found out that it was, of course, 'Ali ؓ, the one who was called the Lion of God. He was very sick at the time with a painful infection in his eyes. He could hardly see when he answered the Prophet's ﷺ call. The Prophet ﷺ kissed 'Ali ؓ on the eyes and his pain went away. Then the Prophet ﷺ clothed him in his own armor and belted his own sword around his waist. He handed him the banner of Islam, kissed him on the forehead, blessed him and said, "Enter with the blessings of Allah."

Inside the fortress the people of Khaybar, to show their confidence and defiance were celebrating the marriage of the son of their chief. All night they had been partying and boasting. When the young bridegroom approached his bride she had told him proudly that she would not remove her veil for him until he had killed the leader of the Arabs encamped before the gates of the city. In the morning the bridegroom shouted down from the high walls of his city challenging the Muslim commander to single combat. 'Ali ؓ answered his challenge and the two met outside the locked gates of the city. The people of Khaybar watched from atop the walls while the Muslim army gathered around.

'Ali ؓ gallantly offered the young bridegroom first strike. The young man struck with his sword and managed to split 'Ali's ؓ shield. 'Ali ؓ in turn wrestled the youth to the ground and kneeling on him to hold him down prepared to deal him a final blow. At this moment the bridegroom spit into 'Ali's ؓ face. 'Ali ؓ stood up letting the boy free. The young man rose to his feet in amazement. He asked 'Ali ؓ what had happened, why had he let him go just at the moment he could have ended his life? 'Ali ؓ explained to the young man that the Muslim soldier fights for Allah and His Prophet ﷺ. He does not fight for wealth or position in this world. He does not fight out of anger or hatred. In fact, the Prophet ﷺ had told them never to do anything in a state of anger. When the young man had spit in his face 'Ali ؓ had felt the anger rise up inside him, and so he had put down his sword. He would not dishonor the Prophet's ﷺ sword by striking in anger.

The bridegroom stood unmoving in his surprise and awe. Never had he heard such words. Never had he seen such honor and courage and devotion to an ideal. He asked 'Ali ؓ to let him take the Prophet's ﷺ hand and become Muslim; then they could execute him. 'Ali ؓ replied that once love for Allah and His Prophet ﷺ had entered the boy's heart, he ceased being 'Ali's ؓ enemy but instead became his brother. 'Ali ؓ called out, *"Allahu Akbar,"* and the boy took *shahada* from him there on the battlefield while his family watched in disbelief from the walls.

After a long battle the fortress of Khaybar finally fell to 'Ali ؓ and the Muslim army. The wife of one of the fallen enemy leaders told the Prophet ﷺ

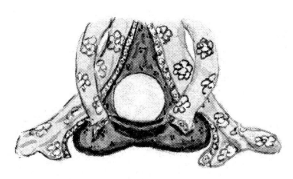

that she had had a dream the night before that the moon had fallen into her lap. Her name was Safiya ؓ and she was a princess of Khaybar. The Prophet ﷺ understood from her dream that she was meant to be a Muslim and one of his wives. She saw the light of Prophethood shining from his face and accepted Islam and married Muhammad *Rasulullah* ﷺ.

The battle of Khaybar was won. The Prophet ﷺ forgave the Jewish tribes of Khaybar. He let them stay in their houses, keep their vast treasures and farm their land. He asked only that a portion of the harvest be sent to Medina every year to help feed the needy among the Muslims. The people of Khaybar rejoiced and thanked God for the generosity and gentleness of Muhammad ﷺ.

There was one woman, however, who had a plan for revenge. She was Zaynab, the widow of one of the Prophet's ﷺ greatest enemies. In an appearance of reconciliation she invited the Prophet ﷺ and his companions to a feast at her house. She prepared a whole roasted lamb into which she injected a terrible poison. The Prophet ﷺ took a piece of meat and began to chew. The meat itself was given a voice and called out to him to tell him it was poisoned. He spit it out immediately and shouted to his companions to stop eating. The Prophet ﷺ became sick but recovered quickly. His companion, Bishr ؓ, who had swallowed a piece of the meat, died the next day. They accused Zaynab of attempting to murder the Prophet ﷺ. Her answer was that if in fact he was really a prophet he would know that the meat was poisoned and would not be killed. If, however, he was a liar, as her people thought, then he would die and they would be rid of him. The Prophet ﷺ forgave her. In his last illness, however, he said that he could still feel the effects of the poison she had fed him.

26

The Mothers of the Believers ﷺ

The Prophet ﷺ was not like other men. In the Quran Allah says to him:
Truly you have a great and powerful nature. (68:4)
His strength, his patience, his understanding, his capacity to love were greater
than that of twenty ordinary men. In addition there was a connection between
him and the natural world. He could hear the animals, the trees, and even the
stones praise their Lord and speak to him. Where he walked the hard ground
became soft to cushion his foot and the soft sand became firm to support his
foot. 'Aisha ﷺ had noticed that when there was thunder or strong wind, she
could see the weather changes reflected in his face. At least once when it began
to rain, he took off his turban and his shirt to feel the rain against his skin. From
his light both the natural and the human world were created and it was as if the
whole world also existed inside of him.

The Prophet's ﷺ household had grown considerably since his arrival in
Medina. He had taken thirteen women in all to be his wives. All of them were
exceptional people of strong commitment and great spiritual gifts, each in her
own way.

The Prophet's ﷺ first wife was, of course,
Khadija al-Kubra ﷺ, Khadija the Great. She was the
mother of all his living children and during her life
he had no other wives. The Prophet ﷺ continued to
remember her with love and thankfulness his whole
life. In fact, of all the wives she was the only one for
whom 'Aisha ﷺ felt jealousy, even though she was
no longer living. After she died the Prophet ﷺ

married Sawda ﷺ. She was an elderly widow, loving and kind, who knew how to run his household and mother his young children.

With the move to Medina the Prophet ﷺ took the young daughter of Abu Bakr ﷺ as his wife. She was the only one of his wives who had never been married before. Sawda ﷺ received her as a daughter and was happy for her company. The Prophet ﷺ would spend alternate nights in their houses until Sawda ﷺ, who was old, gave her night to 'Aisha ﷺ. 'Aisha ﷺ was beautiful and extremely intelligent. Many of the Hadith we know today came through her. The Prophet ﷺ, when asked whom he loved most in the world, often answered, "'Aisha" ﷺ. She was strong willed and playful and absolutely devoted to the Prophet ﷺ. It was only in 'Aisha's ﷺ apartment that the Angel Jibra'il ﷺ would visit the Prophet ﷺ with revelation. On at least one occasion Jibra'il ﷺ sent his greetings to her also.

The Prophet ﷺ also married Hafsa ﷺ, the daughter of 'Umar ﷺ, after her husband died. This made 'Umar ﷺ very happy. She was strong and forceful like her father. Hafsa ﷺ was close in age to 'Aisha ﷺ and they were glad for each other's company and became good friends. She memorized Quran, as did 'Aisha ﷺ. The bits of paper and leather on which the newly revealed verses were written, were placed in her care. She became the guardian of the Quran.

The Prophet ﷺ also married Zaynab bint Khuzayma ﷺ who was famous in Medina for her kindness and charity. She was known as Zaynab ﷺ, mother of the poor. After her husband died and no one asked her to marry, the Prophet ﷺ took her into his household. She died after only eight months.

Umm Salama and her husband Abu Salama had become Muslim in the beginning in Mecca. They were among the first to go to Abyssinia on the Prophet's orders. They returned in time to follow the Muslims to Medina. Abu Salama died of a wound he received at Uhud. The Prophet sat sadly and prayed for him as he lay dying. Umm Salama was only in her late twenties and still very beautiful, but she said she never wanted to marry again. Before he died, Abu Salama told her not to say that. Maybe Allah would send her someone better. When the Prophet proposed to her she understood and accepted. He took care of her and her children by Abu Salama so they would not be orphaned. She moved into Zaynab's house. She gave us almost four hundred Hadith.

The Prophet had married his second cousin Zaynab bint Jahsh to Zayd. She agreed to the marriage only because she could not deny the Prophet anything he asked of her. In her heart, however, she loved only the Prophet. She was quite heartbroken to be married to Zayd but she kept this a secret and did her best. Her marriage to Zayd was not happy for either of them and they divorced. Then Allah informed His Prophet that Zaynab was already his wife in the Highest Heaven. In great joy Zaynab came to join the Prophet's household.

The Muslims after a battle had captured some of the tribe of the Bani Mustaliq, among them Juwayriya, the daughter of their chief. She was very beautiful and the Prophet asked her to marry him. She agreed. Before the marriage was celebrated, the father of Juwayriya arrived. He brought some fine camels to pay her ransom. Two of them, however, were so fine that he could not bear to part with them. He hid them in a small valley on the way to Medina. The Prophet asked him immediately about those missing camels. As a result of this miracle the father became Muslim. As a gift to the new bride of the Prophet the companions released all one hundred families of the Bani

Mustaliq they had taken captive. 'Aisha ﷺ said that no woman was of greater blessing to her people than Juwayriya ﷺ.

At the same time the Prophet ﷺ sent the letter to the Negus of Abyssinia he proposed to one of the Muslims living there in exile. Her name was Umm Habiba ﷺ and she was the daughter of Abu Sufyan ﷺ, who at the time was still an unbeliever. She escaped the persecution of her family by moving to Abyssinia. There her husband had left her and she had stayed on alone, firm in her faith. She was so joyful at the proposal of the Prophet ﷺ that she took off all her jewelry and gave it to the one who brought the news. She came back to Medina to live with the Prophet ﷺ.

The Prophet ﷺ also married Maryam ﷺ, the Christian slave girl sent by the Muqawqis. She gave birth to Ibrahim ﷺ, the Prophet's ﷺ only child born to other than Khadija ﷺ. But Ibrahim ﷺ died before he was two.

The Prophet ﷺ married Rayhana ﷺ who was a member of the Jewish tribe, the Bani Qurayza, after she became Muslim. He married Safiyya ﷺ after the battle of Khaybar. Some of the believers who had lost loved ones in battle were unkind to Safiyya ﷺ and spoke insultingly to her. When she came to the Prophet ﷺ in tears he told her how to reply to them. He said, "Tell them you are of the family of the Prophet Harun ﷺ and that you are the wife of the Prophet Muhammad ﷺ." She became a close friend of 'Aisha ﷺ.

Later when he returned to Mecca he married one more woman, Maymuna ﷺ. She was the aunt of Khalid ibn al-Walid ﷺ and had never left Mecca, even though she had secretly become Muslim. She was widowed and had kept her faith steady in her heart all alone.

The wives of the Prophet ﷺ did not have an easy life. In the early years they were extremely poor with very little food or clothing and absolutely no luxuries. Many of them had grown up in noble families with wealth and servants. When they came to Medina they had nothing. Often there was little to eat but a crust of bread and some dates. When there was food it came naturally from the field. They had to work hard grinding the grain into flour to make bread. They did all the serving of the many guests of the Prophet ﷺ. They worked until their arms and their backs ached. In addition, men and women were always coming to them to ask favors and advice. They served the community of believers with few complaints.

When the Muslims began to become wealthy the Prophet ﷺ maintained his simple lifestyle. While other Muslim wives got bigger houses and servants and new clothes and jewelry, for the wives of the Prophet ﷺ nothing changed. The Prophet ﷺ wore his clothes until they ripped and then he patched them himself. He slept on a mat on the ground. He stored in his house only enough food for that day and if he and his family did not eat it he gave it away to those who had less. He expected his wives to live as simply as he did. Sometimes it became hard for them and they complained to him. But when given the choice to leave and so live in more worldly comfort, they all chose to stay with the Prophet ﷺ and follow his example. Their only desire was 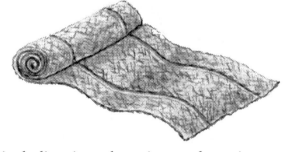 to please Allah and His Prophet ﷺ. For their dedication, devotion and service all the Muslims treated the Prophet's ﷺ wives with the love and respect they showed their own mothers. Allah, in the Quran, addresses the wives of the Prophet ﷺ as, "Mothers of the Believers."

All the grown children of the Prophet ﷺ were born to Khadija ﵂. The older daughters Zaynab ﵂, Umm Kulthum ﵂ and Ruqayya ﵂, had all married and had children but none of these children lived to have children of their own. Only Fatima ﵂ and 'Ali ﵄ had three boys and two girls, the two oldest of which went on to have their own children and grandchildren.

The first to be born to Fatima ﵂ was al-Hasan ﵄, meaning the good one. The next year another son was born who the Prophet ﷺ named al-Husayn ﵄, meaning the little good one. The Prophet ﷺ also loved Zayd's ﵄ son, 'Usama ﵄,

as his own grandson. He delighted in having them sit on his lap and play with him. He even allowed them to climb on his back while he prayed. The Prophet ﷺ loved them all most dearly. They grew strong in the light of his love.

As they grew older the Prophet ﷺ appointed one companion to teach them their religion and to read and write. His name was Dihya ﷺ and he was the most handsome of men. The Angel Jibra'il ﷺ, when he wished to keep company with the Muslims, would take on the appearance of Dihya ﷺ. One day, al-Hasan ﷺ and al-Husayn ﷺ saw their teacher sitting with their beloved grandfather, Muhammad ﷺ. They began climbing all over him searching his pockets for the sweets he usually brought for them. This time, however, it was actually the mighty Archangel Jibra'il ﷺ into whose lap they climbed. He looked with some distress at the Prophet ﷺ, wondering what in the world the boys were looking for. When the Prophet ﷺ explained, Jibra'il ﷺ smiled and made some sweets appear in his pocket as well.

27

The Conquest of Mecca

After the Treaty of Hudaybiyah many people and their families became Muslim. Khalid ibn al-Walid ﷺ and Amr ibn al-'As ﷺ, who had brilliantly led the armies of the non-believers, now entered Islam and used their military skills on the side of Allah and His Prophet ﷺ. It was a heavy blow to the Quraysh to lose their hero and their general.

One year later the Muslims returned to Mecca for the pilgrimage as promised in the Treaty. The Quraysh had left the city. From their hiding places in the hills they watched as wave upon wave of believers entered the sacred area around the Ka'aba chanting, *"Allahu Akbar."* Following the lead of their beloved Prophet ﷺ they circled the Ka'aba seven times. The last three times they ran in order to show

Quraysh that the rumor that the air of Medina had weakened them was entirely false. They performed the *'Umra*, or lesser pilgrimage, because it was not the right time of year to make *Hajj*. After three days they returned peacefully, as they had promised, to Medina.

In the year that followed there was one major battle. Heraclius, the emperor of the Byzantines, who had initially wanted to accept the Prophet's ﷺ invitation to Islam, now decided to obey the advice of his counselors. He

approved the amassing of a great army of one hundred thousand men and sent them to destroy the Muslims. The Prophet ﷺ sent Zayd ؓ to meet them with an army of three thousand one hundred believers. The two sides met at Mut'a in what is now Jordan. The Muslims were completely outnumbered. They were

a tiny force against the enormous, well-equipped army of the Greeks. But the Prophet ﷺ had sent them so they faced their enemy with courage and steadiness.

Zayd ؓ led the first charge. When he fell Ja'afar ؓ, 'Ali's ؓ brother, took the Muslim standard and fought until he also was martyred. Abdullah ibn Rawaha ؓ took the Muslim flag and gave his life. Seven other peerless companions were martyred as they each took the flag. The Muslim army was badly shaken.

Finally Khalid ibn al-Walid ؓ took charge of the Muslim army. He reorganized them and due to his strategy the Byzantine army drew back, thinking the Muslims had received reinforcements during the night. Khalid ؓ at this point counseled that they accept the standoff and leave in order to fight another day. The Byzantines also withdrew, never to return. The Muslims marched back to Medina and Khalid ibn al-Walid ؓ received the title of *Sayfullah,* Sword of Allah, for his courage.

Back in Medina the Prophet ﷺ was given full knowledge of the events at Mut'a. A vision of the battle spread before him like a movie. His eyes filled with tears when he saw his beloved companions fall. The companions around him sobbed with grief as they heard the tale of the battle. They could do nothing but wish they were there to help their friends.

After Hudaybiyah the Muslims had been free to make alliances with whomever they wanted. Some tribes allied themselves with the Quraysh and

some with the Muslims. When they became allies they agreed to support each other. If one were attacked the other would come to their aid. Now it happened that people from a tribe allied with Quraysh ambushed members of a tribe allied with the Muslims. They did it with full knowledge of the Quraysh, right in Mecca itself. The friends of the Muslims took refuge in the Holy Ka'aba because whoever enters there should be safe. Their pursuers violated the holiness of the Ka'aba and killed them. The Prophet ﷺ was angry. He offered the Quraysh a choice. They could pay the families of the victims compensation for the murders and dissolve their alliance with the murderers. Or they could consider the Treaty of Hudaybiyah broken and resume war with the Muslims.

Abu Sufyan ؓ was sent to negotiate with the Prophet ﷺ. He entered Medina without being seen and went straight to his daughter's house. His daughter, Umm Habiba ؓ, had become one of the Prophet's ﷺ wives. She allowed him to enter but when he tried to sit on the mat on which the Prophet ﷺ usually sat she pulled it out from under him. He was startled. She let him understand that she would not

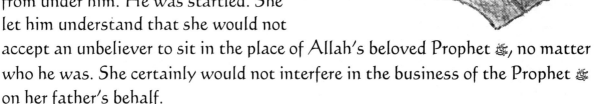

accept an unbeliever to sit in the place of Allah's beloved Prophet ﷺ, no matter who he was. She certainly would not interfere in the business of the Prophet ﷺ on her father's behalf.

Abu Sufyan ؓ went to Abu Bakr ؓ and to 'Umar ؓ and then to other leaders of the *Ansar* and *Muhajirin*. No one would accept to bring him and his proposal to the Prophet ﷺ. Finally 'Ali ؓ suggested he announce his plan at the mosque after prayer and then leave. He did this and returned to Mecca. The Quraysh laughed at him for coming back with nothing and began to prepare for war. It was time to end the injustice that ruled in Mecca and to clean Allah's House from the idols of false belief. The Prophet ﷺ began to prepare for war. In the eighth year of the *Hijra*, the tenth of the month of *Ramadan*, the Prophet ﷺ set out from Medina with ten thousand men. Along the way he was joined by two thousand more. They marched until they were close to Mecca at Mar al-Zahran and there they camped. The Prophet ﷺ ordered each man to collect wood and build a fire so that the light of the flames could be seen all the way to

Mecca. The Quraysh shivered with fear as they imagined the huge army that required so many campfires.

The Prophet's ﷺ uncle, 'Abbas ﷺ, brought his family now to join the Prophet ﷺ, and they were counted as the last *Muhajirin* for their short *hijra* from Mecca to Mar al-Zahran that night. Abu Sufyan ﷺ went to Mar al-Zahran to try to do something to save his people. He happened to meet 'Abbas ﷺ and together they went to the Prophet ﷺ. 'Umar ﷺ wanted to execute Abu Sufyan ﷺ for he had been the leader of the enemy that had caused so much grief and loss of life. But the Prophet ﷺ stopped him. In the morning, after a long night of deliberation, Abu Sufyan ﷺ declared, "*La ilaha ill'Allah*," there is no god but Allah. However, he could not yet pronounce the sequel and declare that Muhammad ﷺ was His Prophet. 'Umar ﷺ was pacing up and down outside the tent aching to punish this enemy of Islam. He was muttering to himself about all the crimes for which he would like to make Abu Sufyan ﷺ pay. On hearing the stormy mutterings of 'Umar ﷺ, Abu Sufyan ﷺ finally pronounced, "*wa Muhammadur Rasulullah*." Abu Sufyan ﷺ was Muslim only by the word of his mouth. Islam had not yet entered his heart. The Prophet ﷺ wanted him to see that when Allah orders something to be, there is no one who can stop it. He asked 'Abbas ﷺ to take Abu Sufyan ﷺ up the hill to a place where he could watch the whole Muslim army pass by.

From this vantage Abu Sufyan ﷺ saw the entire Muslim army pass before him. First came the Bani Sulaym under the command of Khalid ibn al-Walid ﷺ. When they had drawn up close to Abu Sufyan ﷺ they turned and shouted with one voice, "*Allahu Akbar*," until the earth vibrated. Next came Zubayr ibn al-'Awwam ﷺ holding the banner of the *Muhajirin*. They also stopped in front of Abu Sufyan ﷺ and with one voice called out, "*Allahu Akbar*," until the heavens echoed. Then came the Bani Ghifar and the cavalry of the Bani Ka'ab, the archers of Muzayna, and the foot soldiers of the Bani Lab. The Ashja and the Jubayna followed, both of them tribes that had been enemies of the Muslims until very recently. Now they marched together with one voice and one desire to serve Allah and His Prophet ﷺ.

Abu Sufyan ؓ was speechless. Then the Prophet ﷺ came riding up on his blessed red camel, Qaswa, his black turban wound about his noble head, heavenly lights sparkling around him. In front of him Ibn 'Ubada ؓ carried the banner of the *Ansar*. To his right rode Abu Bakr as-Siddiq ؓ and behind them the army of the Helpers of Medina. They stopped and with one tremendous shout that echoed through all the Heavens and Earths they called *"Allahu Akbar,"* Allah is the Most Great.

Now Abu Sufyan ؓ was overwhelmed by the power and majesty of what he had seen, but he did not yet realize that he was not witnessing the display of worldly power but rather the manifestation of the power of Prophethood. This power makes millions of hearts beat faster in love, and millions of eyes shed tears of joy, and millions of men lay down their lives if asked to do so. Even to this day there are tens of millions who have never heard the Prophet's ﷺ sweet voice or looked upon his shining face yet they love him with all their hearts. Minarets all over the world resound with his name and his praises. Pilgrims travel thousands of miles to visit his resting place or to touch something that he touched. What could inspire such love and devotion among those who have never even met him except the power of his Prophethood, Muhammad *Rasulullah* ﷺ.

After watching the entire army pass by Abu Sufyan ؓ was allowed to return to Mecca. He went straight to the Ka'aba and told his people to lay down their arms. There was no way they could win a battle against the mighty Muslim force that was entering their city. The Prophet ﷺ had told him to announce that anyone who entered the area of the Ka'aba or anyone who stayed locked inside their house or the house of Abu Sufyan ؓ would not be harmed.

Only Ikrima ؓ, the son of Abu Jahl, led an armed band to attack the Muslims. He fought with the men of Khalid ibn al-Walid ؓ. Two of his party

died and the rest fled. The Prophet ﷺ had commanded the Muslims not to fight unless they were attacked so the rest of the army marched without incident to the Ka'aba.

The Prophet ﷺ in his black turban that symbolized Majesty began to call out *"Allahu Akbar."* All his companions joined in until even the pebbles on the ground vibrated with the sound. He stood up on the threshold of the Ka'aba and faced the people. He said, "Let everyone expect goodness from me, and know that I was sent as a mercy to the worlds. Islam covers up all the badness which came before it, therefore you are all free."

Then he instructed 'Ali ﷺ to clean the Ka'aba of all its 360 statues and false gods. The Prophet ﷺ recited:

> *The truth has come and falsehood has vanished away.*
> *Surely falsehood is ever certain to vanish.* (17:81)

With these words he and 'Ali ﷺ toppled the statues one by one. There were some remaining on a high shelf out of reach. The Prophet ﷺ asked 'Ali ﷺ to stand on his shoulders, but 'Ali ﷺ begged the Prophet ﷺ to instead stand on him. At this the Holy Prophet ﷺ smiled and said that the whole of creation rested on him. 'Ali ﷺ would never be able to carry all that weight. So 'Ali ﷺ obeyed and climbed upon the Prophet's ﷺ shoulders. When he looked up he found himself gazing at the Divine Throne on a level with the head of the Prophet ﷺ. As he bent forward he saw the layers of the Seven Heavens on a level with the Prophet's ﷺ chest. When he looked down he saw all the Earths on a level with the Prophet's ﷺ blessed feet. He finished cleaning the inside of the Ka'aba and climbed down.

Then the Prophet ﷺ circled the outside of the Ka'aba seven times followed by the Muslims. Bilal ﷺ gave the *adhan* and the Prophet ﷺ led them all in prayer. Then he gave a *khutba* sermon. He told them all to remain firm in their worship of Allah, the One God. The worship of idols handmade of clay or wood or stone was finished. Allah had made true His Promise. The light of

Islam had overcome the darkness. All evils of the past were forgotten. All blood feuds and hatreds forgiven.

He told the people that they must abandon their false pride and arrogance. All men descend from the same father, the Prophet Adam ﷺ, who was made of humble clay. Allah had then made his children, men and women, black and white, of many cultures and languages so that they could try to live together in peace. They must know that they are like one spirit in a variety of different bodies. All people are equal before God. He reminded them that the real purpose of their lives is to find their way back to connection with their Lord, propelled by the force of their love.

As he stopped speaking all those in the crowd were silent. They had fought this man, tried to kill him and his companions. They had driven him from his home, made life miserable for him and those he loved. If they had won they would have killed him and all his followers without mercy. Now he told them clearly they were all forgiven without exception, whether or not they accepted Islam. They had never imagined that a man could be so generous and kind.

The Prophet ﷺ went to sit on a high place on the rocks of Safa. First the men and then the women came one by one to take *ba'yat;* to take his hand and swear obedience to Allah and His Prophet ﷺ. The worst enemies now came to be forgiven and accepted as brothers and sisters in Islam. Even Ikrima ؓ, who had fought against the Muslims that very day, declared his Islam and asked for forgiveness. Ikimra ؓ further vowed that whatever he had spent in energy and wealth to fight against Islam he would now try hard to double in the cause of Allah. The Prophet ﷺ then prayed for Allah to accept Ikrima's ؓ vow and He did.

28

The Battle of Hunayn

Following the submission of Mecca the tribes of Arabia entered Islam in great numbers. It became obvious to everyone that Allah was describing these events when He said in the Quran:

When the help of Allah and victory come,
Then you will see men entering Allah's religion in crowds. (110:1-2)

Most of the companions rejoiced. Only Abu Bakr ☀ was deeply saddened. He said that it was also decreed that a time would come when the opposite would occur. Just as at that time crowds of people raced each other to embrace Islam, so the time would come when they would leave Islam in equal numbers. When that time came a man could live from morning to evening as a believer and from evening to morning as an unbeliever.

Even the allies of Quraysh came quickly to the Muslim side. Once the door opened everyone rushed to get in. Some entered with their whole hearts and some, at first, with only their words, but their hearts were soon to follow. Only one tribe, the Hawazin, continued in their opposition to the Prophet ☀. They amassed a large army of twenty thousand soldiers in a valley outside of Mecca called Hunayn. The leader of the Hawazin was Malik ibn Awf ☀. He insisted, against good advice, that all their women and children, tents and herds be stationed at the edge of the battlefield. In this way he felt he was insuring that no man would turn and run. They would either achieve their goal or die trying.

The Prophet ﷺ assembled his defenses. On the seventh of *Shawwal*, in the eighth year of the *Hijra*, over twelve thousand fighting men followed the Prophet ﷺ, mounted on his mule, Duldul. Two thousand of these came from Mecca, some of whom had not yet left idol worship to accept Islam. The others were new Muslims, and as they admired their apparent strength their pride expanded. They began to boast that nothing could stand between them and victory. Khalid ibn al-Walid ؓ led a contingent of young soldiers who in their pride and youth refused to wear any armor for protection. The Prophet ﷺ warned them that their attitude was arrogant and tainted with unbelief. Victory is Allah's and He gives it to whomever He wishes. They were relying on their own strength rather than on their Lord.

Khalid ibn al-Walid ؓ led the first foray. The arrows of the Hawazin

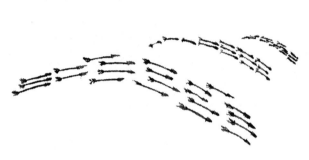

rained down on them and they wavered. As the enemy calvary charged they turned to flee, forcing line upon line of the Muslim troops behind them to retreat also. Those who had only recently become Muslim panicked and the whole army fell into disarray. Only the Prophet ﷺ remained unmoving.

Alone without anything but the protection his faith provided, he faced the attacking warriors of the unbelievers. Heaven and Earth were in stunned silence and the Divine Throne trembled.

The Holy Prophet ﷺ faced the enemy with the whole majesty of his Prophethood and his full reliance on Allah. He announced to them his presence and his challenge. Then he told 'Abbas ؓ to call out with his booming voice that soared above the noise of the battle, "O People of the Tree, come here!" Both the *Ansar* and the *Muhajirin* answered his call and came running to the side of their Prophet ﷺ. The Prophet ﷺ prayed to Allah. Then he threw a handful of pebbles into the faces of the advancing enemy, as he had done at Badr. Allah sent an Angelic army that was only visible to the Hawazin. They saw white men riding spotted horses, the very sight of whom caused uncontrollable fear. Together these forces pushed forward into the oncoming enemy, until they drove them back. The Hawazin turned and ran. They ran past their women and their children. They ran past their tents and their fine herds of camels and sheep. They abandoned everything and ran until they took refuge in the walled city of Ta'if. After laying siege for several weeks the Muslims, on the order of their Prophet ﷺ, let the men of the Hawazin live.

The Muslims now had won a great fortune. They had captured thousands of women and children with their tents and jewelry and all their belongings. They had captured in addition thousands more livestock, sheep, goats, and camels. The Prophet ﷺ divided up the wealth among all the warriors. Many of the tribal leaders had entered Islam only in order to become rich and powerful. The Prophet ﷺ began to satisfy their desires. Abu Sufyan ﷺ and his family were rewarded with three hundred camels and one hundred and twenty ounces of silver. Others received two hundred camels and many ounces of silver. Every soldier received four camels and forty sheep, but the ones who received by far the most wealth after the battle of Hunayn were the Meccans.

There began to be some bitter, jealous grumblings among the *Ansar* of Medina. The Prophet ﷺ called them to come to him. He asked them if it were not true that when he had first arrived they were killing each other, unable to make peace, praying to idols, not knowing Allah or His worship? Had they not been poor and in darkness? The *Ansar* began to weep, for they knew without doubt that what the Prophet ﷺ said was the truth. They answered that he spoke correctly, and they thanked Allah for all that had been given to them.

Then the Prophet ﷺ gently told them that they could have answered otherwise. They could have said to him, "O Muhammad ﷺ you came to us poor and outcast. We welcomed you and gave you a home. You were alone and we supported you. You were called a liar and we believed in you." The *Ansar* now

began to feel as if their hearts were on fire. The Prophet ﷺ continued, "O people of the *Ansar*, others will take home camels and sheep and goats, but you will take home Muhammad *Rasulullah* ﷺ." At this the strong men of the *Ansar* had hardly enough strength left to breathe. They cried until their beards were wet. When at last they were able to speak, one and all asked to be forgiven for their momentary envy of worldly wealth. In reality, with all their hearts, they wanted nothing more than to have the Prophet ﷺ of Allah as their portion to take home to Medina.

The Hawazin sent word to the Prophet ﷺ asking for mercy and for their families to be returned to them. Among the captives was Shayma ﷺ, whose mother, Halima as Sa'dia ﷺ, had been the nurse of the Prophet ﷺ. The Prophet ﷺ welcomed her with joyous emotion and sat her beside him on a blanket. She had been the baby for whose benefit he had refused to drink from Halima's ﷺ left side. The Prophet ﷺ and the Muslims set free all the captives of the Hawazin. Their chief, Malik ibn Awf ﷺ, in response to this generous act, became Muslim.

The Prophet ﷺ and his companions returned to Medina. During the ninth year of the *Hijra* many old enemies came to take his hand. One of them, Ka'b ibn Zuhayr ﷺ, had been a poet responsible for writing some of the most vicious and terrible poems about the Prophet ﷺ. Poems were like the newspapers of that time. They spread from mouth to mouth, in this case spreading lies among the unbelievers. Ka'b ﷺ now entered Medina and accepted Islam. He began to recite a poem in praise of the Prophet ﷺ and Islam. The poem was so beautiful that the Prophet ﷺ rose to his feet and began to whirl. In his whirling his cloak slipped to the ground. Afterwards he draped this cloak over the shoulders of Ka'b ﷺ. This poem came to be called the *Burdah*, or the Cloak of the Prophet ﷺ, and is still recited today all over the Muslim world.

In Constantinople, the Emperor Heraclius was considering how to end the threat posed by the Muslims. Word began to spread that he was assembling an army to attack Arabia again. The Prophet ﷺ on hearing the news began to

collect his own forces. His wives donated all their jewelry to be sold for food and weapons. Abu Bakr ؓ gave every single thing he owned to his beloved Prophet ﷺ. 'Uthman ؓ and 'Umar ؓ contributed fortunes.

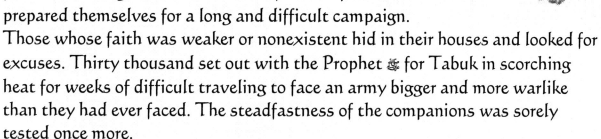

It was the middle of summer and fiercely hot in the Arabian desert. The wells of Tabuk where the army of Heraclius was gathering were far away. Those whose faith was strong answered the call of the Prophet ﷺ and prepared themselves for a long and difficult campaign. Those whose faith was weaker or nonexistent hid in their houses and looked for excuses. Thirty thousand set out with the Prophet ﷺ for Tabuk in scorching heat for weeks of difficult traveling to face an army bigger and more warlike than they had ever faced. The steadfastness of the companions was sorely tested once more.

When they reached Tabuk the wells were almost dry. In another miracle the water welled up at the Prophet's ﷺ touch and the whole army drank. They marched on a ways, but nowhere did they see the enemy or any trace of him. The Prophet ﷺ rested two weeks at Tabuk during which time many tribes came to see him and become allies. The Muslims returned without incident to Medina.

It was the time of pilgrimage once again. The Prophet ﷺ sent Abu Bakr ؓ to lead the Muslim pilgrims to Mecca. The unbelievers still came to the Ka'aba at *Hajj* time to make their own idolatrous worship, which sometimes included circling the Ka'aba totally naked. During this *Hajj* a new verse of Quran was revealed to the Prophet ﷺ. He sent 'Ali ؓ to announce that from that time on, unbelievers were forbidden to perform *Hajj* or enter the Ka'aba. They, however, had nothing to fear from the Muslims and they were allowed to complete their rituals that year. The idol worshippers were so impressed by the conduct of the

Muslims that many of them accepted Islam right then and there. The bright light of Islam had reached its fullness and it illuminated even the darkest regions.

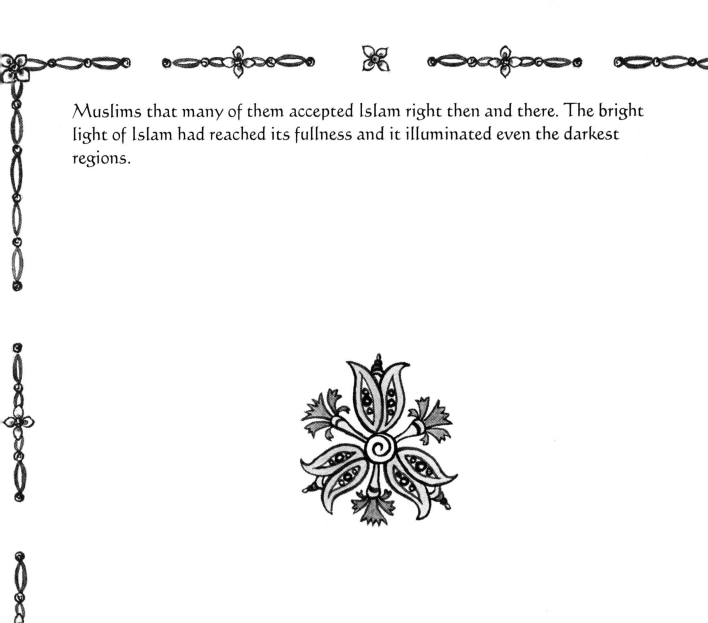

The Passing of the Prophet ﷺ

In the tenth year of the *Hijra* there finally seemed to be peace. Envoys came from all over to see the Prophet ﷺ, hear his message, and pledge their allegiance. Messengers even came from as far away as China. The emperor of China had asked them to bring back a painting so that he might gaze upon the blessed face of Allah's Prophet ﷺ. Although the Prophet ﷺ discouraged the painting of faces or figures, he wanted to grant the emperor his wish. He called for a piece of leather and focused his attention on it so strongly that his blessed features began to appear on its surface. He folded the leather and ordered the envoys not to open it until they reached their emperor in China. When the Emperor unfolded the leather he saw the Prophet's ﷺ beautiful face reflected there until, little by little, it dissolved into air and disappeared. He accepted Islam as did his messengers.

In this year the Prophet ﷺ announced his intention to go to Mecca for pilgrimage. Everyone wanted to go with him. People began streaming into Mecca from all sides. The *Hajj* fell that year in March and the day of *'Arafat* was on a Friday. The Prophet ﷺ entered the *Haram as-Sharif*,  the enclosed area around the Ka'aba, by the door of the Bani Shayba. He asked Allah to increase His House in honor and respect. They made their *tawaf*, circling the House seven times, after which they ascended the hill of *Safa*, praising and glorifying their Lord. They descended and walked quickly to the nearby hill of *Marwa*. Doing this seven times they completed the *sa'i*. Just at that moment 'Ali ؓ arrived with a large caravan from Yemen and joined the pilgrimage.

There were forty thousand pilgrims who gathered to hear the Friday *Khutba* sermon on the day of *'Arafat*. The Prophet ﷺ spoke movingly about the rights of women and orphans. He reminded the *hajjis* to avoid wrong actions, especially taking advantage of women and children. On the Day of Judgment there will be no pardoning of these two sins in the Divine Presence. He asked the believers to live together as brothers, to respect each other's families and property, and not to take usury. He told them that it might be that they would not see him again in this place. They must hold tight to two things he was leaving for them, the Quran and his *Sunnah* (his example). He warned them that if they strayed from the path outlined by these two it would result in their downfall.

From Mecca the Prophet ﷺ moved on to Mina. There he threw stones at three symbols of *Shaytan* as Ibrahim ؑ and Ismail ؑ had done. The *hajjis*

followed, pledging themselves to fight their lower selves that encourage us to do the things that Allah dislikes. The Prophet ﷺ gave another khutba at Mina reminding the *hajjis* that blood feuds had been abolished and that they must obey their leaders so long as their leaders obeyed the Quran. He went on to describe the Last Days when Good and Evil will wage war.

At the end of this sermon he asked them: "O people, have I delivered my message? Have I made my mission clear?" From the thousands of hearts that heard his question came the same sincere answer: "Yes you have, O *Rasulullah* ﷺ." The Prophet ﷺ raised his hands asking his Lord to bear witness. After this he said, "Whose friend I am, 'Ali ؏ is also his friend. O Allah, be the Friend of him who is 'Ali's ؏ friend and the Enemy of him who is his enemy and help him who gives 'Ali ؏ help." He told the people to repeat what he had said to their friends and neighbors who were not able to be there.

At this time a new verse of Quran was revealed:
Today I have perfected your religion for you
And I have completed My blessing upon you,
And I have approved Islam for your religion. (5:3)

Only Abu Bakr ؏ and a few others understood the meaning. The Prophet's ﷺ work was completed, his mission accomplished. He had delivered everything that was revealed to him, in word and deed. Nothing was missing or left in doubt. Allah would take him soon to the world of the unseen because his time in this difficult and dirty world was coming to an end. Abu Bakr ؏ wept.

The pilgrims made their farewell *tawaf* and the Prophet ﷺ left Mecca for the last time. As the palm trees of Medina came into view he greeted them with joy. It was not long after this that he fell ill.

The Prophet ﷺ had a high fever and was unable to lead the prayers. He asked Abu Bakr ؏ to be the Imam in his place. Abu Bakr ؏ wept as he stood to lead the believers in the night prayer. The next morning the Prophet ﷺ felt a little better. He entered from the door of his house that adjoined the mosque. Seated he followed the believers in the prayer. After the prayer he asked Allah to bless him and his community of prophets and believers. He told the people to protect their belief and to keep to his way. Then he told them a short story about an unnamed servant of Allah who was asked, "Which do you love more, this

world or the world to come?" The servant answered that he loved the world to come. His Lord was very pleased with him and promised him a place in His Almighty Presence.

Nobody understood the underlying meaning of this story except Abu Bakr ﷺ. Tears began to well up in his eyes for he knew that the servant of Allah was in fact the Holy Prophet ﷺ and that he had chosen the Afterlife over this life. The Prophet ﷺ turned to Abu Bakr ﷺ and reassured him that they would be together again soon. He went on to say that if he could have taken any friend other than Allah Almighty, he would have chosen Abu Bakr ﷺ as his friend.

He reminded the people that death is a necessary part of life. If any of them had claims on him or if he owed them anything they should speak. He wanted to leave this world cleanly with nothing left undone. One companion named 'Ukkasha ibn Mihsan ﷺ spoke up. He said that one day he had been riding near the Prophet ﷺ just as he raised his stick to urge on his camel. The Prophet's ﷺ stick had hit 'Ukkasha ﷺ by mistake and hurt him. Now 'Ukkasha ﷺ wanted justice. The assembly of companions gasped in horror. The Prophet ﷺ, however, gave his stick to 'Ukkasha ﷺ and told him to strike. But 'Ukkasha ﷺ continued that when the Prophet ﷺ had hit him his skin had been bare. So the holy Prophet ﷺ removed his cloak until his side was bare. He asked softly that 'Ukkasha ﷺ not hit him too hard because he was still weak and sick. The companions begged 'Ukkasha ﷺ to hit one of them instead but 'Ukkasha ﷺ took the stick and stepped up to the Prophet ﷺ. Then he knelt down and buried his face against the Prophet's ﷺ skin like a little child against its mother. Tears came to the Prophet's ﷺ eyes. The companions wept. Even the mosque sighed and groaned in love. The Prophet ﷺ prayed for 'Ukkasha ﷺ and Allah granted his prayer.

After this the Prophet ﷺ retired to his room. By the third day his illness had become so bad that he could no longer sit up. He said that he felt the effects of the poisoned lamb that Zaynab had given him at Khaybar. Those companions who came to see him he blessed, and gave instructions for his burial

and funeral. He told them he would be waiting for them on the other side. Even if they could not see him he would see them and be asking Allah's Mercy for them and His Forgiveness.

At the time of the night prayer he opened the door between his room and the mosque and saw the believers following Abu Bakr ☙ in prayer. He smiled and was content for he knew that after he was gone his nation would continue to follow his way.

'Aisha ☙, in whose room he was staying, brought him a tooth stick and softened it for him. He brushed his teeth and lay down with his head on her chest. The word spread that the blessed Prophet ﷺ was sitting up and feeling better. Many of the companions went back to their homes for the first time in days. The next day, however, he was worse again. Fatima ☙ came in tears to see her father. He told her not to cry for she would be the first of his companions to follow him and that made her smile.

Around noon on the twelfth day of *Rabi' ul-Awwal*, with his head in 'Aisha's ☙ lap, the Prophet ﷺ was heard to say, "*Rafiq ul 'a'la, Rafiq ul 'a'la,* the Friend on high, the Exalted Companion." Then he exchanged this world of sadness for the world of eternal beauty.

'Umar ☙ could not believe that the Prophet ﷺ had really died. He insisted that he had only gone to visit his Lord and would return. Abu Bakr ☙, however, understood. He calmed 'Umar ☙ with these verses of Quran:

> *Muhammad is but a Messenger;*
> *Messengers have passed away before him.*
> *Why if he should die or be killed,*
> *Will you turn about on your heels?*
> *If any man should turn about on his heels,*
> *He will not harm Allah in any way;*
> *And Allah will reward the thankful.*
> *It is not given to any soul to die except by*
> *The permission of Allah, at an appointed time.*

Whoever desires the reward of this world,
We will give it to him,
And whoever desires the reward of the other world,
We will give him of that; and We will reward the thankful.
(3:144-145)

'Ali ☙ and his close companions washed the Prophet ﷺ in his clothes and dug his grave right where he had died in the house of 'Aisha ☙, next to his mosque. All the believers came in small groups, first the men then the women, to pray the funeral prayer and say their last goodbyes. Then they placed him in his grave.

Just as the sun seemed to shine brighter the day Muhammad *Rasulullah* ﷺ had entered Medina, so now on this day the world darkened as if the sun had

set forever. Medina, the City of the Prophet ﷺ, had never seemed so desperately sad and forsaken. Now the believers faced their biggest challenge, to follow the footsteps of the Prophet ﷺ without his loving presence and kindly support.

When the sun sets the moon takes its place and still illuminates the world but with a more subtle light. The Prophet ﷺ had died but he was not really gone. He promised to keep watch over his community in death as he had in life. He promised to ask Allah's Blessing for our good deeds and to ask Allah's Forgiveness for our bad deeds. Although we cannot see him he remains alive in his grave. He hears the greetings and the praises that are addressed to him. When you give him *salams* he returns them many times over. So although we might no longer be able to see him, he continues to watch over us and pray for us. And when our turn comes to cross over the bridge to the other world he promised, God Willing, to be there waiting for us.

In addition to the Generous Quran and his *Sunnah* (his example), the Prophet ﷺ left us another thing to guide us through this world. Whoever has a

dream of the Prophet Muhammad ﷺ it is as if he had truly seen him, for nothing false or ugly can take his shape.

Allah will never leave this world without light. First Allah made the light of Muhammad ﷺ. From that light He made all of creation. It is our task to look for that light wherever we can find it, before and behind us, within and without us, and especially in the faces of sincere and pious believers, and follow it with love and obedience to the end of our days.

Allah said in Quran:
> *And He (Allah) is with you wherever you are.* (27:4)

And He also said in another verse:
> *The Prophet of Allah is with you.* (49:7)

So if we keep our minds and our hearts busy with the remembrance of Allah Almighty and His Beloved Prophet ﷺ, one day, God Willing, we will see the Prophet's ﷺ shining face, and kiss his blessed hand, and rest in the light of his eyes for as long as Allah wills us to rest, hopefully for a very, very long time.

Printed in the United States
86992LV00005B/99-100/A